If you can Write You can Draw

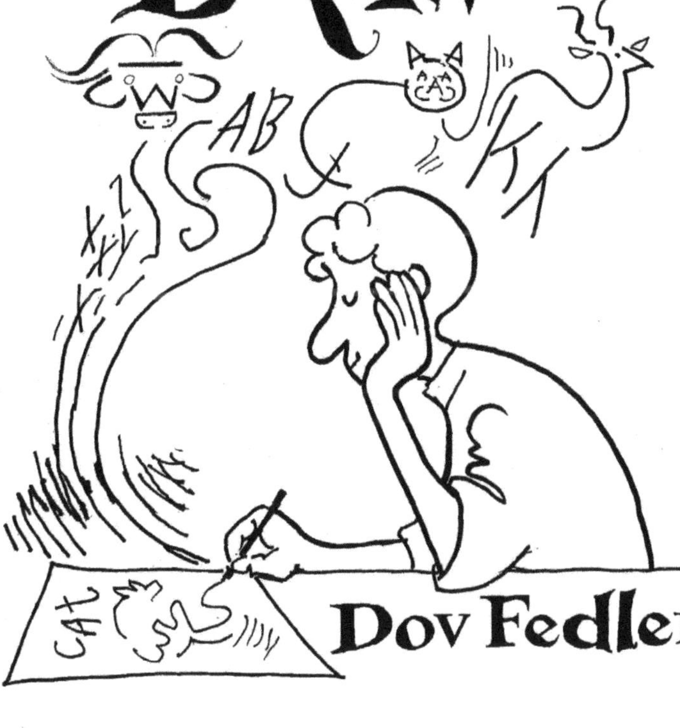

Dov Fedler

First published by Joanne Fedler Media 2018

www.joannefedler.com (publisher's website)
www.marketingmentor.live (design by Nailia Minnebaeva)

Printed in Australia, UK and USA.

National Library of Australia Cataloguing-in-Publication data:

ISBN 978-0-6482838-9-8 (Paperback)
ISBN 978-0-6482838-8-1 (Hardback)
ISBN 978-0-9954063-7-7 (E-book)

Praise for *If You Can Write, You Can Draw*

I have always been fascinated by 'how to draw' books. And heaven knows, there are enough of them. Generally speaking, they mostly suffer from the same error; they become a subconscious vehicle for the artist-author's work and presume a certain level of natural ability from the reader.

Dov has managed to avoid those pitfalls and has produced the first book that I have seen on drawing that tackles the subject holistically. The drawings are delightful and engaging, and because of their sketchy spontaneity make one think, 'But of course, that's it!'

If you want to have a thoroughly enjoyable and eye-opening learning experience, this is the book for you.

John Meyer
Internationally renowned portrait and landscape artist

To my Dad whose dream it was to be an editor.

*To my daughter Joanne for fulfilling it
and becoming mine.*

And to Debbie who saw it all coming from far off.

CONTENTS

1

THE YELLOW PENCIL

I remember the first time I saw a pencil. I was seated in a pram and someone was making marks on a page with a yellow pencil. The next thing I knew, the pencil was turned over and the marks were rubbed out. To my three-year-old eyes, this was sheer magic and it sparked my own creative awakening. Some epiphanies are this mundane.

Not long after, I picked up a pencil and began to draw and I've never stopped (I've been at it for 74 years now). I've even had the good fortune of making my livelihood as a cartoonist for the past 50 years.

To this day I don't know whether the person at the foot of my pram was writing or drawing. At the time I was too small to know the difference. But I've since concluded that I cannot distinguish one from the other. To me, they have always been one and the same: marks on a page that make meaning of some kind, be it serious and profound, or fun and frivolous.

But what was unmistakable in that innocent moment of witnessing was my understanding that *I could also do that.* All I had to do was lift a pencil and put it to paper.

And if I could do it, so can you.

This magical ritual of creation and self-expression is free to anyone who desires it. I wrote this book to show you that drawing is not a secret gift bestowed on the talented few.

It can be yours too, if you want it.

2

WHAT IS DRAWING?

When we say the word 'drawing', we mostly think of holding an instrument in our hand and making a mark on a surface – whether it be on paper, a wall, in sand. That is the artistic extension of drawing but drawing itself is innate to our expression as human beings. We all draw constantly, even though we're unaware of it.

When we gesture *'I don't know', 'He's crazy', 'Come here'*, we move our hands in the air. Think of how you use your hands to describe the size of the fish you caught, how you hold your fingers to show how much wine you'd like the waiter to pour, or how you might demonstrate how big your kid has grown. We raise our eyebrows to indicate surprise; we wink to invoke confidentiality. We crease our faces to describe approval or anger. We all naturally contort our faces to show our emotion: 'The food was disgusting,' we say as we scrunch up our face. 'The play was sublime,' we sigh as we close our eyes dreamily.

We create pictures of ourselves constantly and unconsciously for others to interpret. Gestures are nothing more than spatial drawings that leave no trace.

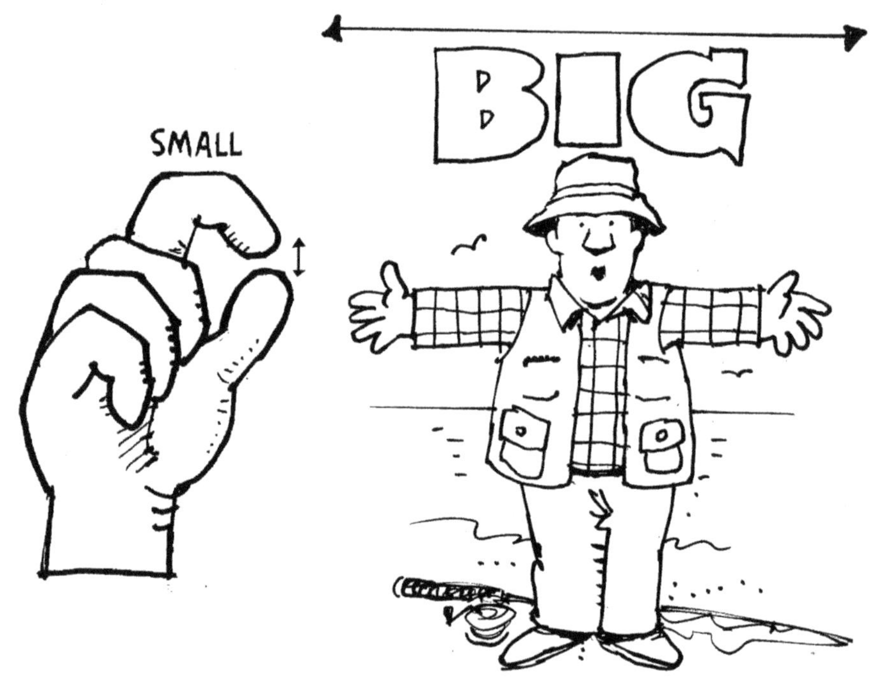

Take a look at these pictures – these simple gestures are 'air drawings'. We use them all the time. They are familiar and easily understandable. These 'drawings' are in fact a universal sign language. Deaf people have mastered this art and communicate using an entire language made up of intricate hand movements and facial expressions. When we gesture, we are automatically drawing. From the air to paper is truly a small step.

Before movies included sound, silent film actors turned gesture into an art. Charles Chaplin and Buster Keaton competed to see who could use the fewest subtitles in their films. Audiences read their expressions as if they were written descriptions. Body language is a form of drawing and most of us understand it intuitively. Just think – if we did not have devices or inventions (like cameras and computers), we'd have to communicate using sketches or gestures.

Drawing is as ancient as human existence. How do we know? Our earliest ancestors drew with implements and inks made from plants on cave walls. Their drawings depicted hunters chasing a food source. The paintings were executed in strategic locations to inform future hunters what prey might be hunted there.

Today, using our smartphones and iPhones, we use emoticons and GIFs to express our feelings – and what are these but modern-day drawings?

Drawing is also a problem-solving device, a way of bringing order to our thoughts. A list of things to do in your diary is a drawing of intent.

But perhaps drawing's most valuable gift is that it leads to analysis and invention, two of our greatest resources as human beings. And isn't our world in need of greater thinkers and problem-solvers given the mess we've made of it? Learning to draw will enhance your thinking.

3

WE ALL START OUT AS ARTISTS

In kindergarten all my classmates drew as feverishly and enthusiastically as I did. That's because drawing – a primary motor skill – is the first outreach of a child beyond herself and the first tangible evidence of contact with the world outside. When children hold a pencil or crayon, they attempt to record what they see. Grabbing a pen or brush excites thought in the human brain in a way it does not in, say, a monkey. All children begin by drawing a circle with radiating lines which is a representation of the sun. They go on to draw figures and objects, portraits of their family and their pets.

Back then I was just like everyone else – we all had it in us to become artists. My gift as a child was not unique, but perhaps I was a little ahead of the game. I saw better, looked more, and never took the magic for granted.

Children are generally encouraged to draw. Until they

are not. As soon as I left nursery school for 'big' school, it was time to put childish things aside – drawing became one of the sins of inattention, of not 'concentrating.' Had I been left to doodle while the teacher spoke, I'm convinced the lessons would have been embedded in my consciousness far more effectively than the methods teachers resorted to. It wasn't drawing that disrupted my concentration: in my day canes and rulers were the weapons of mass distraction.

By the time I got to primary school at the age of six I had acquired a reputation in my family as being something of an artist. I was reproducing images of Churchill, Hitler and Stalin from the newspaper. I also copied the comic characters from the Sunday supplements like Mickey Mouse and Donald Duck. I struggled with Goofy, but knew I would soon get him right.

Once in school I had new material with which to draw: words. I learnt to draw the alphabet and recognised the letters as old friends. I saw immediately that writing was just an extension of drawing, and that drawing is simply an essay of letters.

This is what I want to share with you and is the reason I have written this book.

If you can write, trust me, you can draw.

4

YES, I'M TALKING TO YOU

If you think you have no drawing ability, you are wrong. We all draw before we learn to write. If you can write, you're already drawing. You just don't know it.

My aim is to teach you to use what you already know. Remember when you were a kid? How you drew effortlessly in your first classes? How you finger-painted? Made shapes in the sand tray? Drawing is innate. It's an instinct. But as we get older, we get shamed out of it – unless we're as stubborn or desperate as I was to keep at it.

If you're reading this, you already have an advantage because you can read and write. My method for teaching is founded on one simple principle: if you can write, you can draw. Writing is drawing. And fun.

Drawing follows some geometrical rules, but it is also a visual stream of consciousness as one idea flows into another naturally. That's why a drawing can express your emotional response to a visual stimulus. At its finest and most elegant, we call it art. Or even Art.

But let's not get carried away. Let's be less artsy-fartsy. Drawing is what happens when you put a pen to paper and see what emerges.

Once you begin, it will help you to see better, imagine more and create something new every single day. I want to encourage you to draw, whether it's to create cartoons, think more creatively, make art or produce any other form that excites you.

I have spent my life following the Yellow Pencil Road.

I still do. Please join me on this never-ending journey.

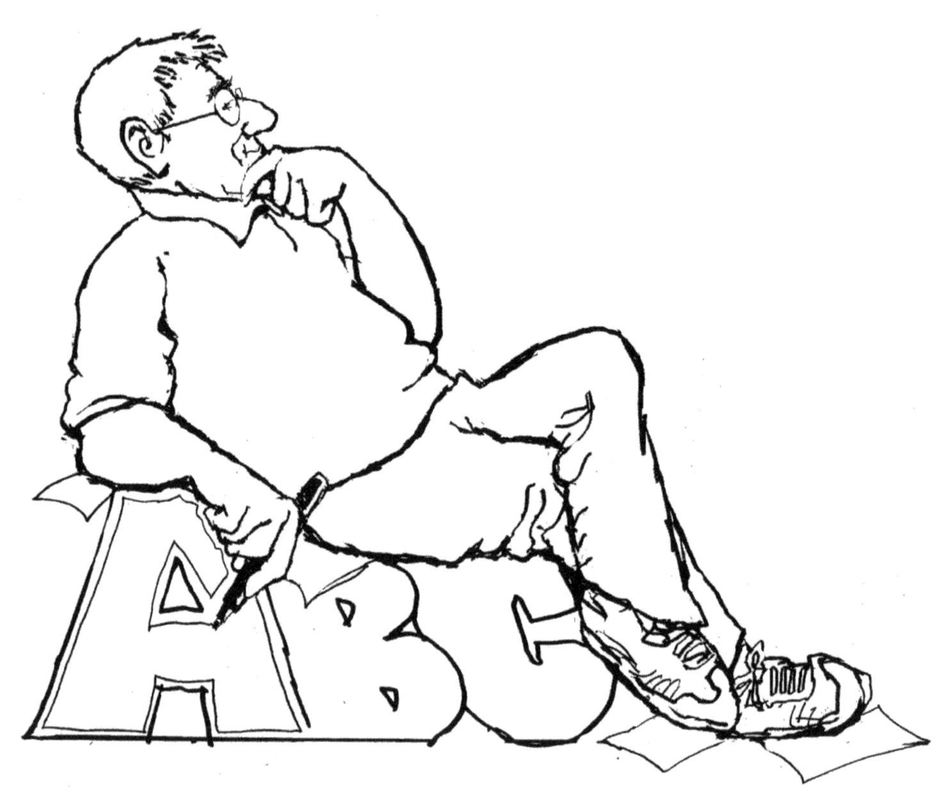
ABC

5

WHY YOU SHOULD

I'm not a big fan of 'should's' – they make everything sound so terminally serious. But in this chapter, I'd like to offer you reasons to draw that might excite and delight you – and if you believe that you 'should' pursue such enterprises that bring you joy, enhance your well-being and bring clarity to your life, well then, maybe you 'should'.

I also don't believe in having too many rules when it comes to drawing. But it helps to have a starting point, which is why I have written this book. Drawing can be simple, even mechanical – like taking a photograph. My aim in this book is to teach you the mechanics, to draw on what you already know, which you can then employ more creatively later on.

Place a pen in your hand, put it to paper, draw any squiggle, and just continue the line. Let it go wherever it may. Draw a circle, enclose it in a square, add some curlicues, draw an eye framed by eyelashes, write your name in block letters, doodle away. *Let the drawing take you for a walk*, as the artist Paul Klee advised. Allow the drawing to happen.

What you'll find is that a mechanism kicks in the moment you begin – it's called thought.

Leonardo da Vinci, one of the greatest artists (and scientists), had an extraordinary imagination. He conceived of flying way back in the late fifteenth century.

At the time it was a crazy notion. He designed the first hang-glider and airplane. His knowledge of drawing enabled his inventions, gave them guts and reach.

Just look at his sketch for a helicopter:

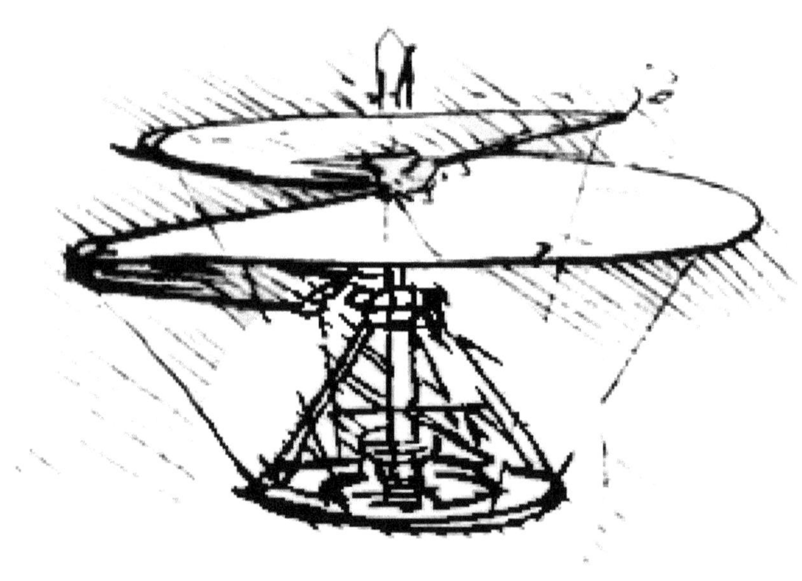

Drawing makes thoughts visible.

Brilliant thinkers think in pictures. Let me prove it to you with another example.

Albert Einstein stunned the world around 1916 with his general theory of Relativity, one of the most important discoveries of the twentieth century. He was a whiz at numbers but what made Einstein unique is that he looked at the universe with a child's eye and asked his question as a picture.

'If I am flying at the speed of light holding a mirror in front of me, will my image reflect in the mirror?'

Don't try to think this out just yet. Draw a small picture so that you can see Einstein's question.

Forget the words for now. The drawing is the question.

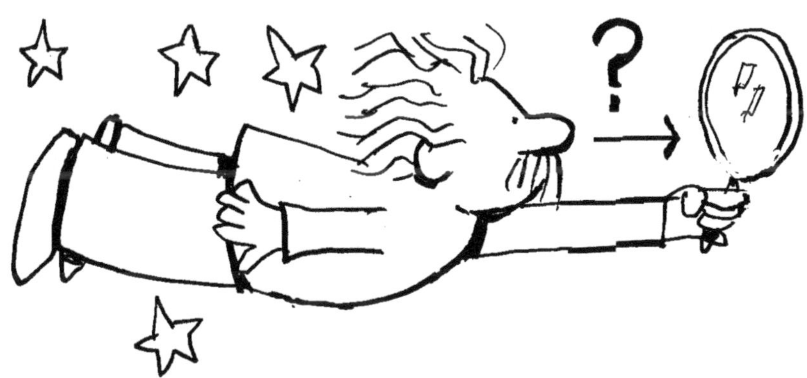

Einstein's thought process went something like this: 'If I am travelling at the speed of light, and the mirror in my hand is travelling away at the same speed, in theory, there should be no reflection. But in fact, there would be a reflection in the mirror because the speed of light is constant.'

Only real scientists and mathematicians understand the science behind the theory but the lesson lies in the simple picture that Einstein presented himself in solving this great cosmic mystery.

Even if you are not trying to crack the codes of the universe, there are so many ways in which you could enhance your life if you make drawing a regular practice. Here are some suggestions:

1. To get clarity on an idea. Drawing makes our ideas or thoughts clearer. Some ideas need to be drawn to be understood before we can turn them into reality.
2. To help structure an argument or process.
3. To design a new product.
4. To explain a process – using diagrams, flowcharts, infographics or maps (think of how doctors will often resort to 'drawing' the organ that needs operating on or to explain a condition we have – and think how much better we'd understand what was wrong with us if they knew the basics of drawing).
5. As a public speaking aid. If you have an important speech to deliver and are nervous about remembering what you have to say, try encrypting the speech with pictograms – use diagrams or drawings as placeholders for a thought instead of words, which can sometimes blur an idea. All you have to do is see the picture to remember the idea. A thought can be packed into one single image. Once you can draw it, you can speak it.

6. To make meaning of an experience or a feeling. One of our unique qualities as human beings is that we interpret all marks in an effort to make meaning. 'What does this mean?' we ask, of just about everything. To a monkey, a drawing of a banana is just a meaningless scribble. Because of the meaning and thoughts human drawings represent, psychologists and educators, such as Edward de Bono, have used drawings as a therapy. Drawing is a channel to our emotions. When we look at the work of the wondrous Vincent Van Gogh, we feel his torment. His paintings reveal that he was anything but a calm soul. If we have a powerful feeling inside us, drawing is one way for us to let it out.
7. To connect with other human beings. If you feel something when you draw, it will be expressed in the marks you leave on a page. And while that is a marvelous balm to our souls, the real joy comes when we share our drawings with others and they feel something too. If we are moved to draw, and are moved in drawing, we will move others.

   One of my greatest cartoons is this one, which I penned on the eve of Nelson Mandela's passing. To this day, I still have people reach out to me, telling me that this brought tears to their eyes. And the truth is, it brought tears to mine when I drew it.

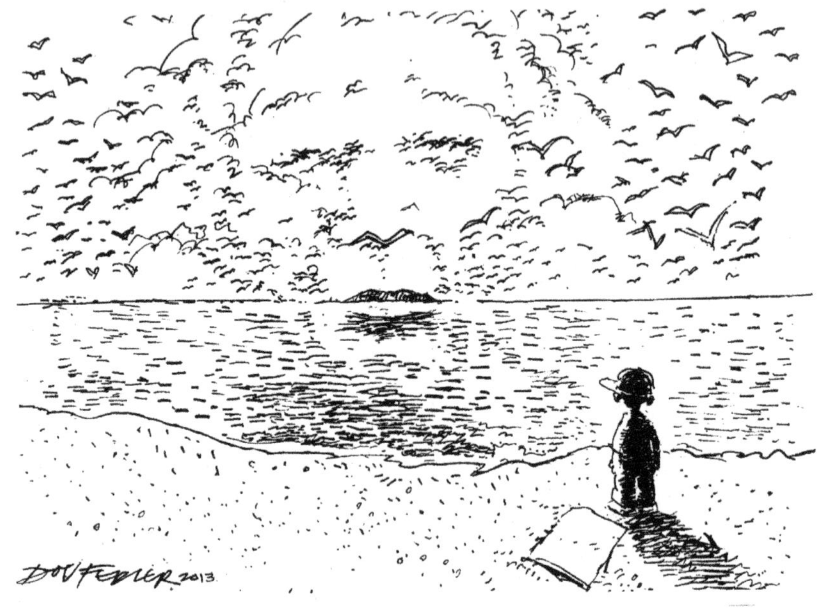

8. For the sheer delight and joy of it. Humans need to draw as much as we need to write – to express ourselves and to make sense of our lives.

There are countless other benefits to drawing. But you'll only really appreciate them once you begin.

When you draw, a new world will open up for you. It certainly did for me.

And if none of this has convinced you, finally, I believe you should learn to draw because you already can.

6

MEASURING THE MISTS

My father wanted me to be a dentist. He saw no future in a life dedicated to the arts. He was both practical and domineering. We reached an uneasy compromise where I agreed to study architecture, since it included a bit of drawing and no sticking of hands into rotten mouths. And what happened? I failed first year architecture, not once, but twice.

Mathematics and physics were subjects that made my years at high school and university utterly miserable. They appeared to be areas of knowledge in a mist-filled void. At university, I finally managed to pass first-year maths and physics, an ancient requirement of the Faculty of Architecture. For the next 20 years I kept the textbook, *Elementary Physics* by Gilbert Stead, on my shelf until I donated it to some hapless charity or flea market. Just before giving it away, I came upon it on my shelf, that cursed bible of the failed wannabe architect. I stopped and looked at this reminder of bad times and asked out loud,

'What the hell *is* physics?' I opened the book and there on page 1 it said, 'Physics is essentially the science of measurement.' Suddenly the mists cleared, and I could see a horizon. I saw forms and shapes. I saw pictures. *Eureka!*

I then began a voyage of rediscovery, and soon I found how and where I had lost my way. It was when I was taught at the outset that 'length times breadth equals area', drummed into me in the abbreviation L x B = A. But how could you take one thing, multiply it by another, and come up with a third thing? Why not Lemons times Bananas equals Apples? That could also be abbreviated to L x B = A. What the hell was 'times' anyway? It had never made any sense to me.

I was over 40 years old when I first truly understood the *common denominator* and the *square unit.* Length and breadth share an identical measuring unit, which can be expressed as inches, centimeters or light years (as long as these measurements belong to the same measuring scheme). An area is a counting of identical squares all added up to make a surface. Multiplication (the dreaded 'times') is just a fast way of counting. This all came to me as a small revelation.

Once understood and committed to memory, L x B = A is easy if we think of the formula in pictures. So: four squares stacked on four squares stacked on four squares equals twelve squares (or whatever the unit is you're multiplying to reach a total).

Drawing is much easier than physics. Let me prove it to you.

Take a pen and paper. Draw an apple, a lemon and a banana as *badly* as you can. Maybe your lemon and your apple look a lot alike, but your banana should stand alone. In some ways, it should resemble the letter **C**, while the other fruits will probably more resemble **Os**. If you can do that, you are already drawing. It is that simple to follow.

My hope is that this will be the only 'textbook' you will ever need to get you drawing. And I promise it won't take 40 years for the penny to drop.

So what happened after my spectacular failure at university? I left the rigid disciplines of designing buildings and escaped into graphic arts. After seven years in the world of advertising, at the age of 28, I ventured out on my own as a freelance cartoonist and illustrator. I became a political cartoonist working for *The Star*, then the largest daily newspaper in South Africa. I did this for 50 years, and from that stable platform served many advertising agencies.

I have yet to have a formal drawing lesson.

7

DRAW A STRAIGHT LINE

Pick up a pen and pretend you're about to write – a shopping list, a Post-it note, a reminder to yourself to pick up your dry-cleaning. I don't even want you to think about a ruler. Forget I even mentioned it.

We're going to draw a straight line freehand. I know you think you can't. But trust me, you can. Draw a line, the width of your thumb, as if you were underlining a word you have written.

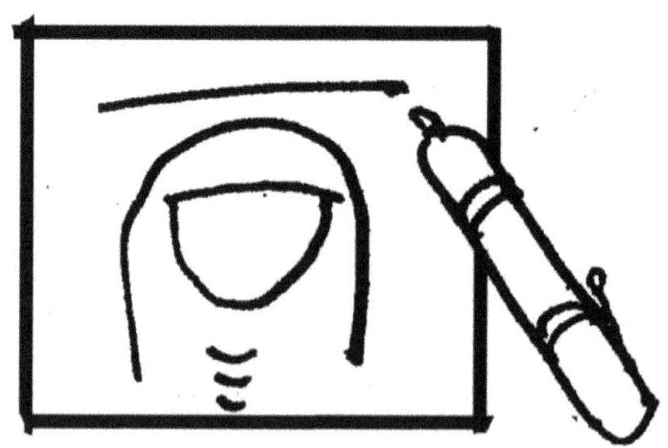

It may not be perfect, but you will manage to draw something pretty straight because of its short length.

Now you are ready to draw a longer line. You can do it. The secret of drawing a straight line is not where you start but where you finish. Think of this secret in visual terms – like this:

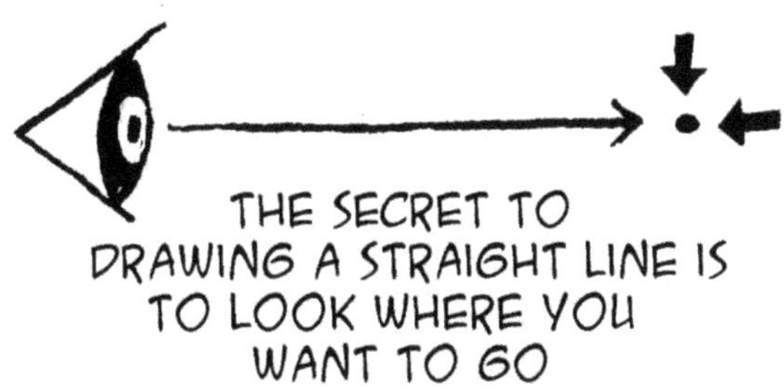

A golfer putting for the cup knows where he has to aim the ball. And drawing is no different.

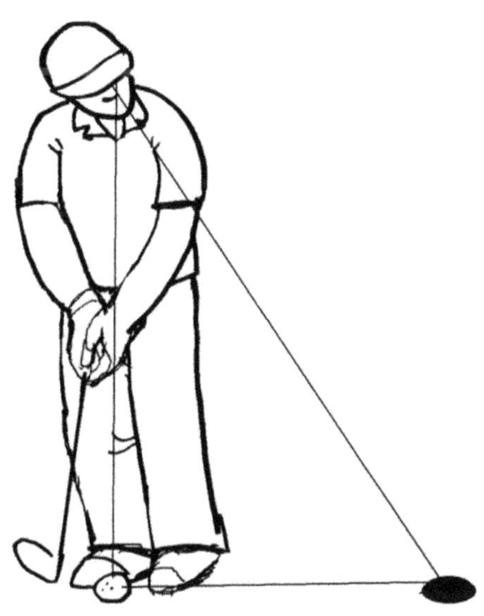

You and the golfer both want to get from *here* to *there* in the most efficient way possible. But think about how a golfer does it: a golfer *takes time when lining up the putt.*

So when drawing a straight line, plot a point where you want the line to end. Shift your focus to the finishing point, which should attract your eye like a magnet. Now simply move the pen towards the dot.

Start with a short distance and increase it as your confidence grows.

The principle is always the same: look where you are headed. Just follow your eye at your own speed. Take your time. There is no rule that says a straight line of, say, ten centimeters has to be drawn quickly. No one will ever know how long it took you to draw your line. Lines are good at keeping these sorts of secrets.

Don't ever be in a rush. Speed doesn't make you draw better.

TAKE YOUR TIME. When you are taking your time, you are thinking. You are focusing.

Focused thought enhances any skill we are trying to acquire.

Now repeat the lesson. Again and again and again and again and again.

The more you draw, the better you will become.

8

THE ESSENTIAL CIRCLE

Examine a selection of coins in your currency. You might pull out coins of different sizes, say 10, 20, and 50-cent pieces. Study them for a good minute or two.

Now put them away and draw a few circles that you estimate to be the same size as your 10c, 20c, or 50c coins.

Don't use pencils and erasers. Use a pen (one that's indelible). I want you to see your 'mistakes' so you can learn from them. What you need is patience and a willingness to manage frustration. An artist's sketchbook is filled with what non-drawers might call failed drawings. But I assure you there is never a failed drawing – each drawing is a stepping-stone to improvement. Please treat all your 'failures' with this in mind.

Draw lots of coins. Now take the real coins and place them over the circles you have drawn. You'll be amazed at how close you can get with just a little practice.

THE SAME RULE APPLIES TO DRAWING A CIRCLE AS TO DRAWING A STRAIGHT LINE. BUT KEEP AWAY FROM THE CENTRE

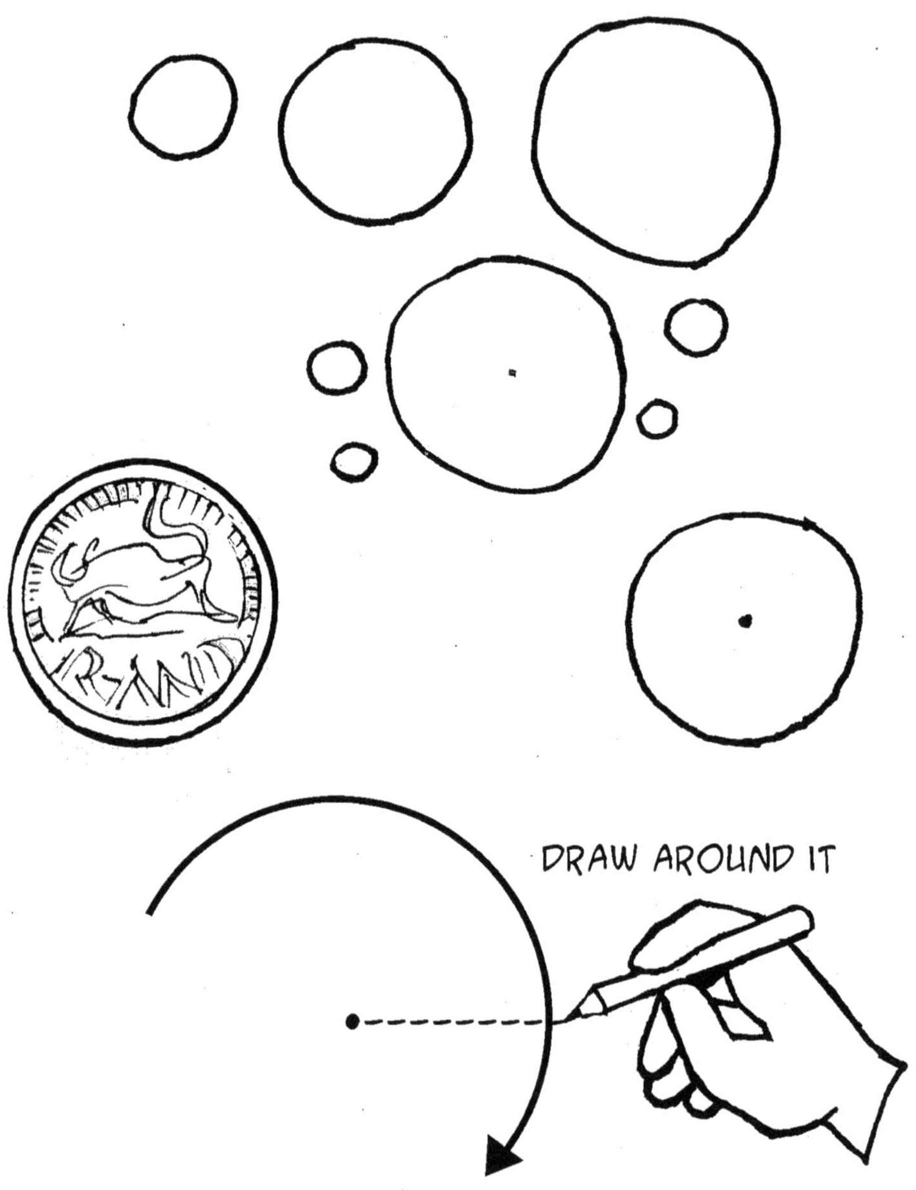

Now ask yourself if you're having fun. Perhaps the main point of drawing is to have fun.

Once you move from straight lines to circles, you've mastered some of the basics. Consider, once again if necessary, what you need and wish to draw – and how far you have already progressed.

Hands are your drawing buddies; drawing is a hand skill. By the way, even if you don't have hands, you can still draw. Many people without hands have taught themselves to draw using their feet or their mouths. So if you have hands, you're at a huge advantage and have no excuse for not drawing.

As for paper and pen or pencil, I'm old-fashioned. Forget computers, smart devices, or other digital thingamajigs. If you want to learn to draw, you have to draw. On the back of an envelope, if you must.

9

YOUR OLD FRIENDS – LETTERS AND NUMBERS

Okay, now that you've mastered the straight line and the circle, you are ready to graduate to something a little more complex. Don't be intimated; we're going to take this slow and steady. And remember, if you can write, you can draw.

You can read the word *Cat*, but probably think you can't draw one, right?

Perhaps not yet. But every time you read a word, you are assembling a number of pictures in your mind. Every letter is a drawing, representing a sound. The word *Cat* looks vastly different to an actual cat.

But since I know you can write the word *Cat*, let's begin right there. Get your pen and paper and write *Cat*. Look at the marks you have made. Right there, you have enough symbols with which to draw an actual cat. See, letters can be more than just parts of a word; they are your writing toolbox.

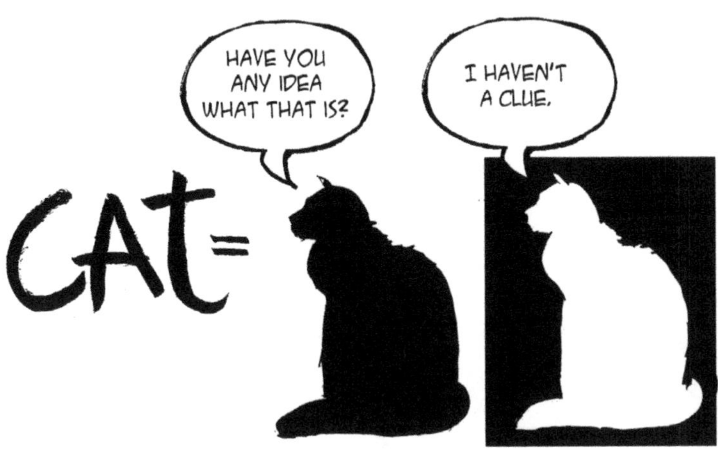

With a **C**, you can draw a cat's head, also its body and cheeks. The capital letter **A** can be used to draw both eyes and a nose. The capital **T** then becomes its whiskers and the lower-case **t** the cat's tail.

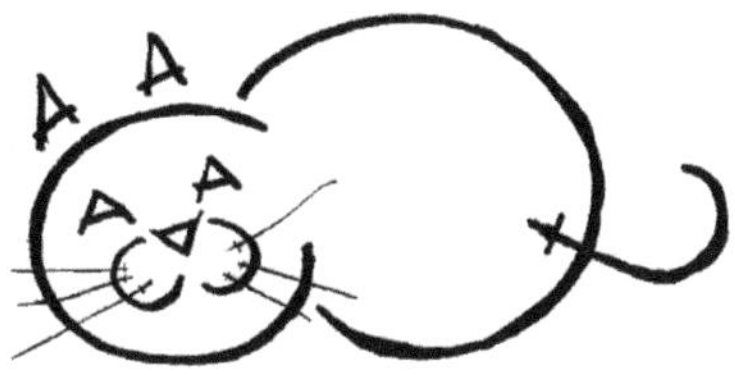

Once you've got the hang of this, you can start to refine your drawing, but for now just have a go at drawing a cat using just the letters in the word *Cat*.

You can also draw a cat using just a few numbers:

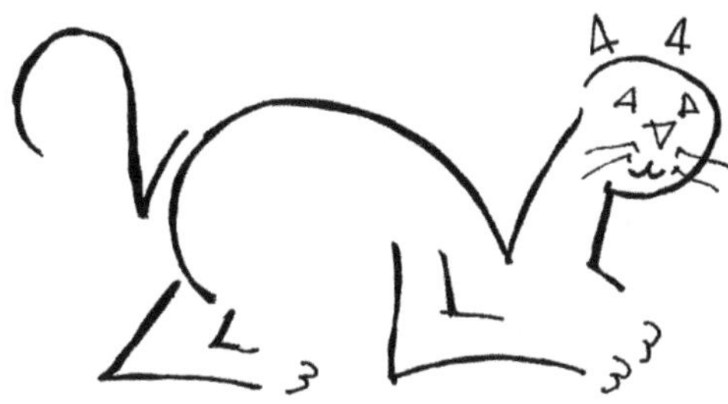

Here are other attempts to draw objects employing the cat-trick.

As you do these exercises, keep expanding the way you recognise letters and numbers.

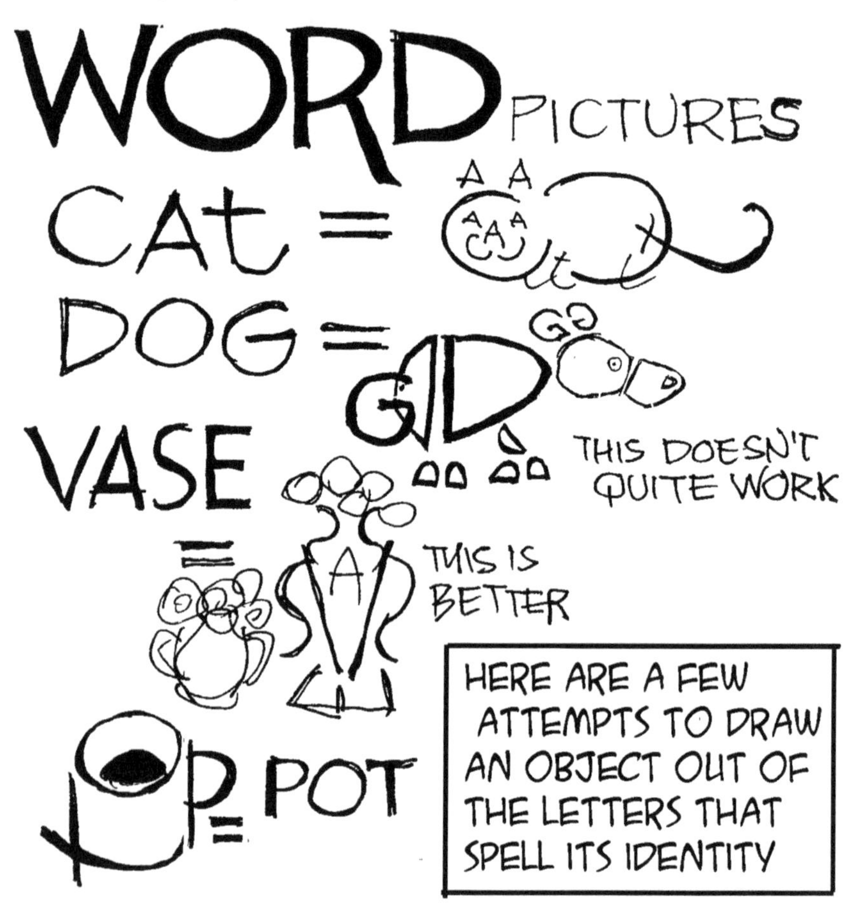

The leap from writing to drawing is easy. All it requires is a shuffling of the skill you have in writing.

There are even more ways to draw a cat and many other animals. Trust that you have everything you need to start drawing.

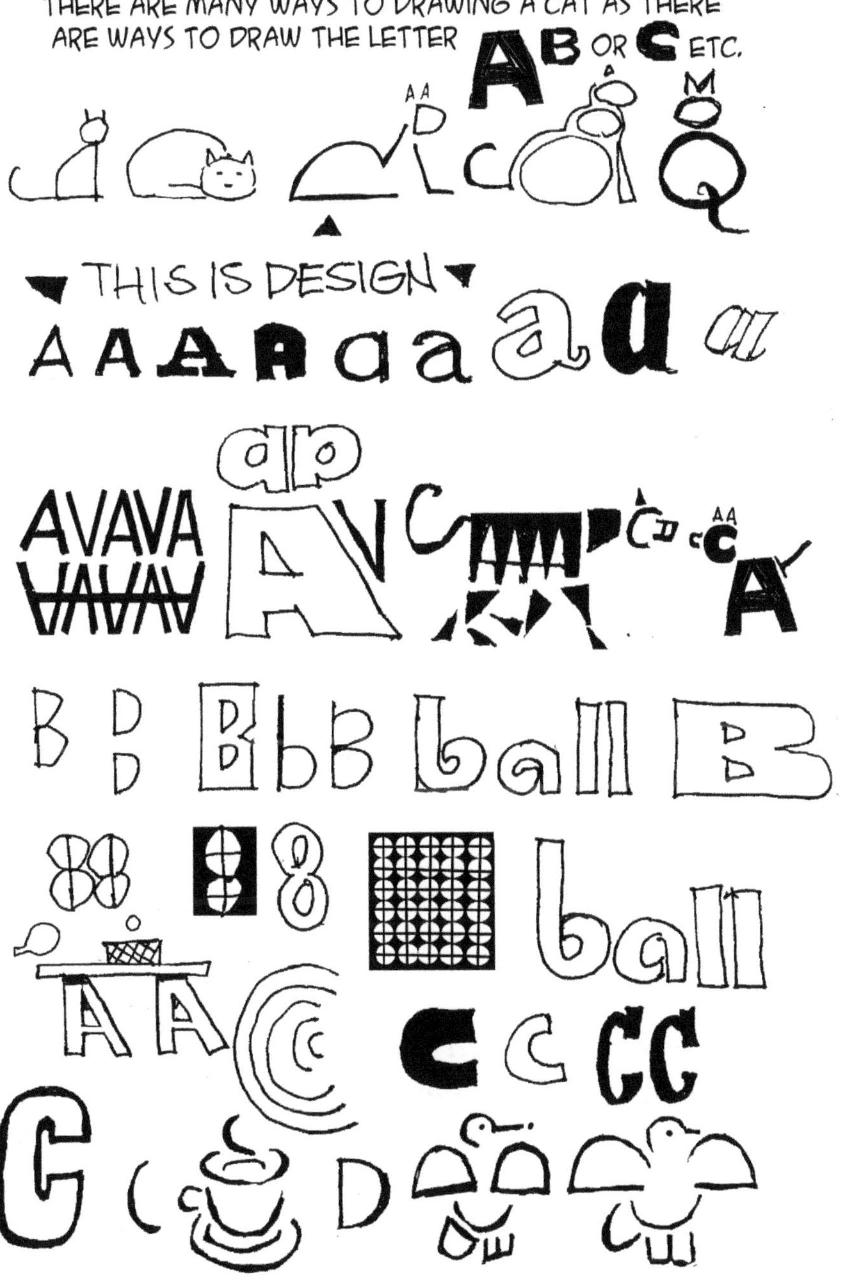

I would go so far as to say that it is in fact easier to draw than to write. A picture shows us what the object is – or is intended to be. Pictures, drawings, are a universal language. We understand them without having to be taught – which is not the case with writing, which is a skill we have to learn.

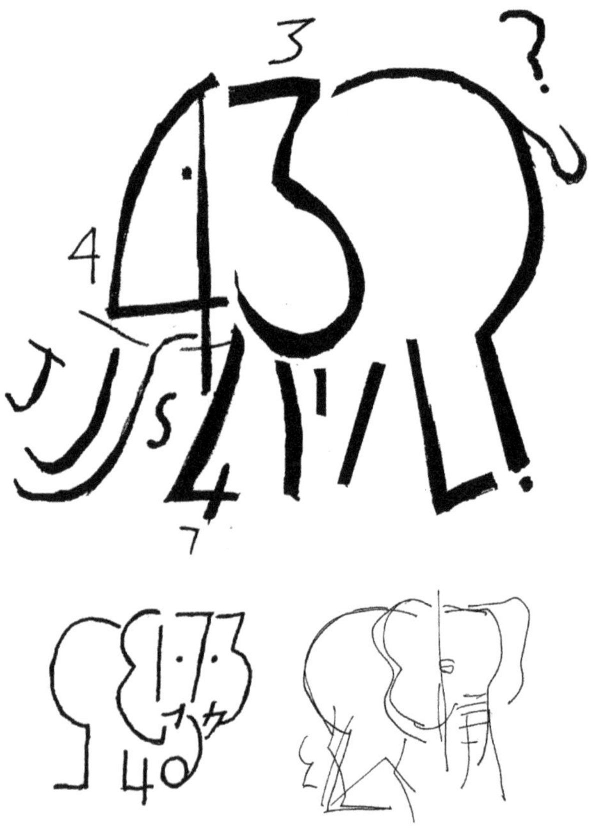

A word – written down – is not, say, two semi-circles placed one on top of another. It has an imposed meaning: the representation of a sound, the noise we make when speaking.

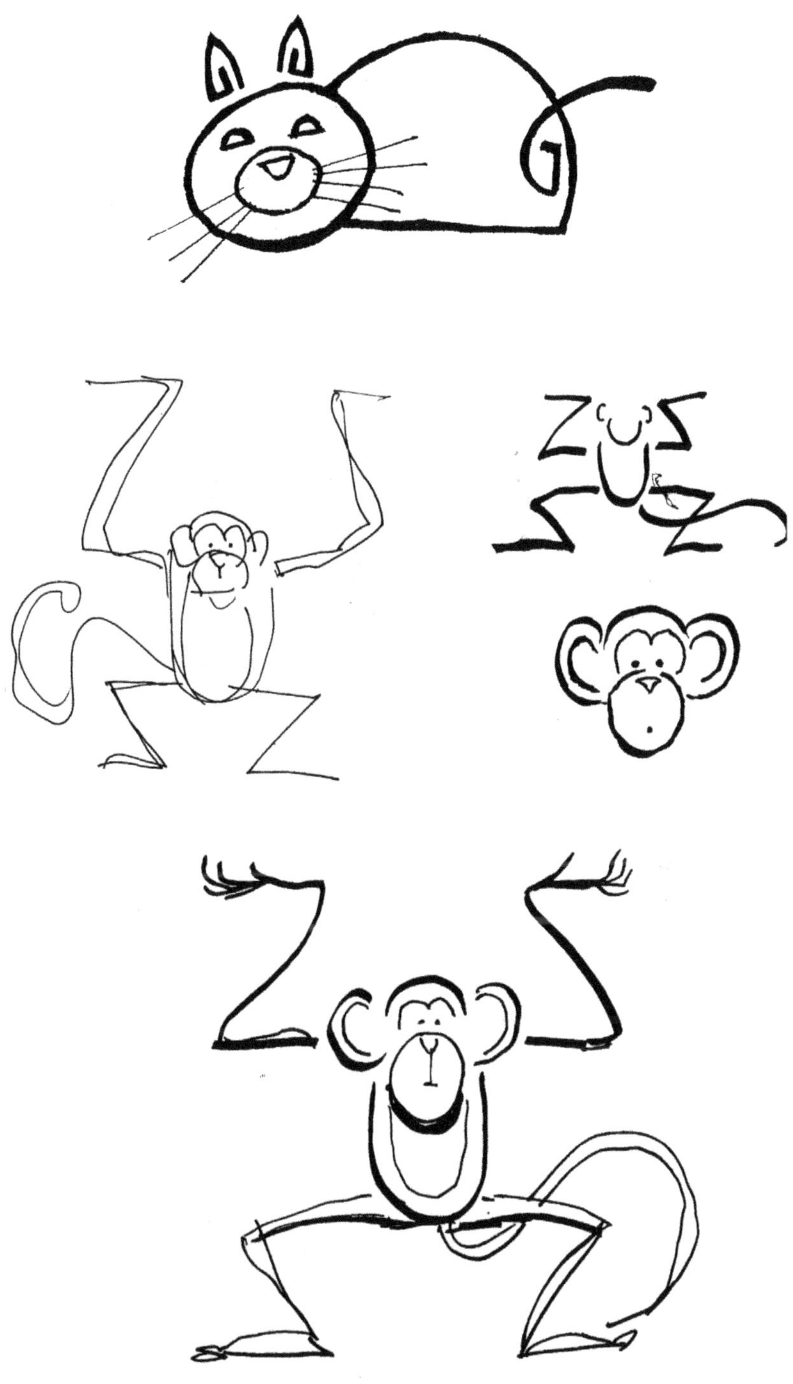

Writing with ease evolves with an ability to draw, and that ability assists us to communicate better. As we learn to draw both letters and pictures, our communication skills expand – and this is essential because as the world moves towards greater use of images, we become more dependent on them.

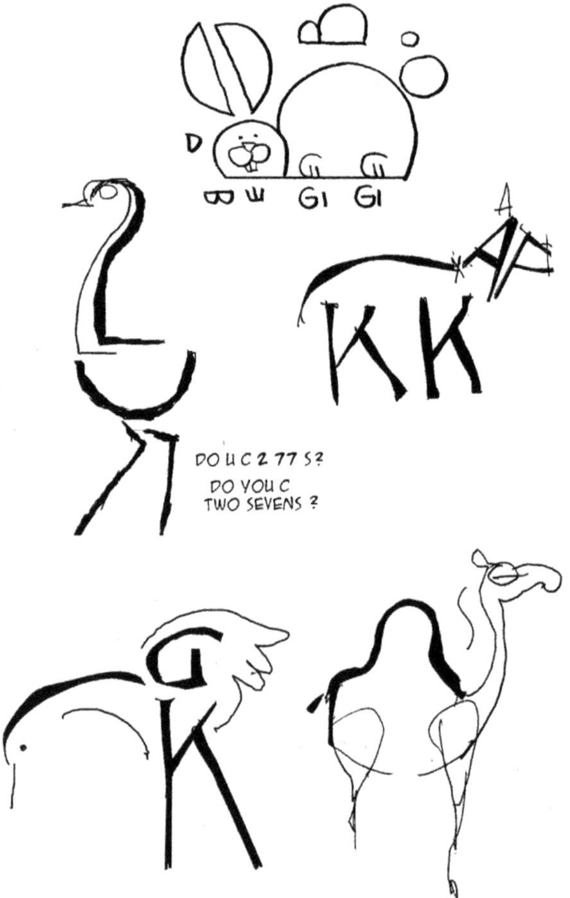

Think of all the emoticons yet to be invented.

Please trust me when I say: the alphabet contains every shape and line you will ever need to draw.

What you may need to develop is the way you look at them and therefore, the way you see them.

10

IT'S NOT HOW YOU LOOK, IT'S HOW YOU SEE

Sometimes we look at things so often we don't really see them at all. We become inured by familiarity.

In this chapter, I want you to look at letters and numbers differently so that you really see them for what they are – your friends, your drawing tools. Just look at the example below – if you reassemble the characters **OWCDMUHH** you can draw Charlie Brown.

Examine the drawing and puzzle it out. You may be struggling to isolate the letter U in the drawing. That's because it's upside down.

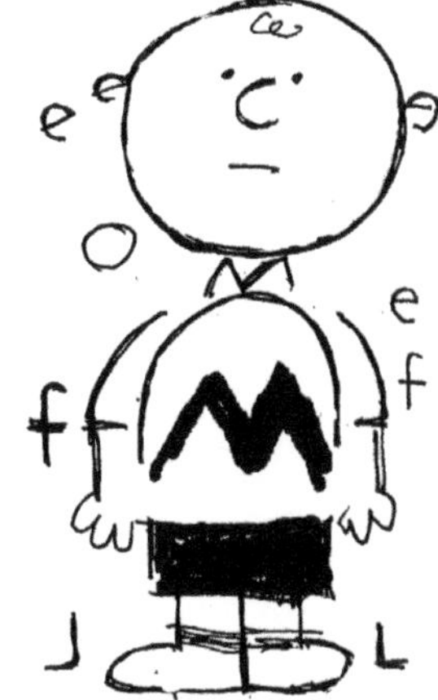

THINGS LOOK DIFFERENT UPSIDE DOWN

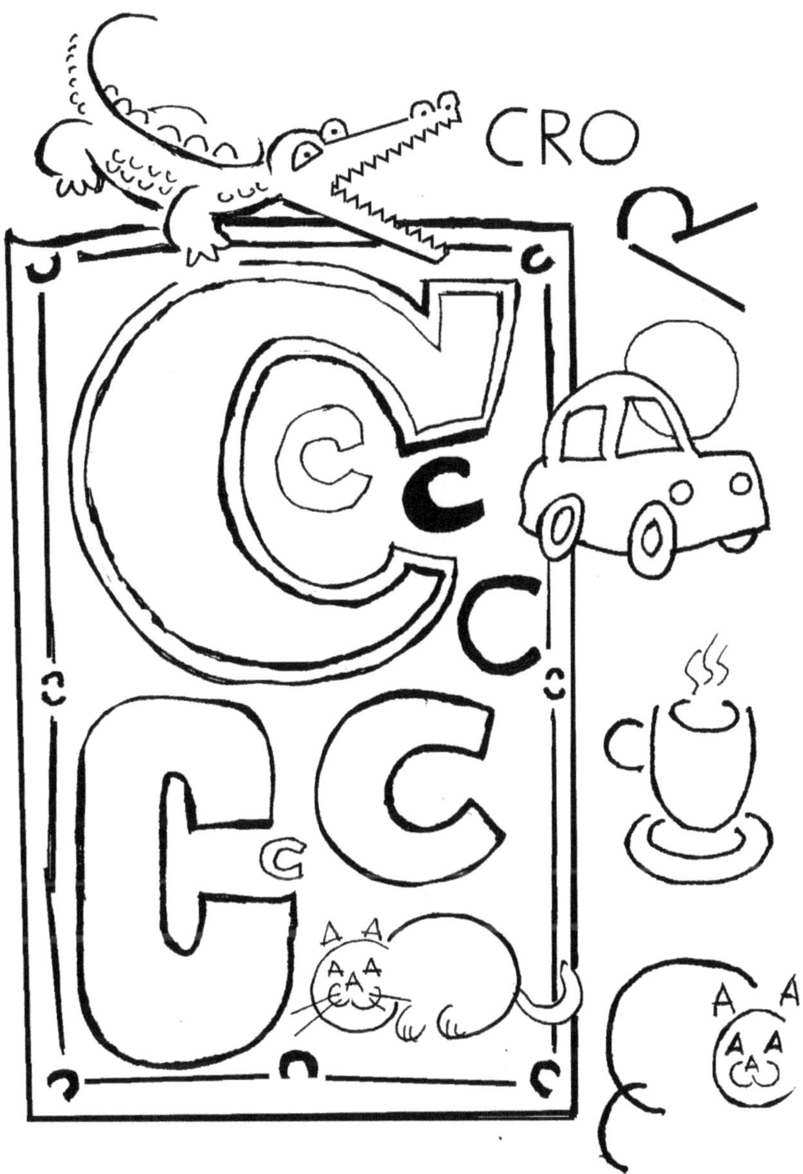

THE MORE YOU PLAY WITH
LETTERS AND NUMBERS AS ELEMENTS OF
DESIGN AND DRAWING, THE MORE YOU
WILL SEE

All creatures see differently – owls, cats and dogs all have their unique way of seeing. We all perceive the three-dimensional world, but humans alone are able to transfer what we see to a two-dimensional plane. We have created drawing, the recording of our experience of the world in pictures. Letters are just such pictures – indeed, a printed page is as much a picture as a drawing.

Here are more examples for you to study and draw:

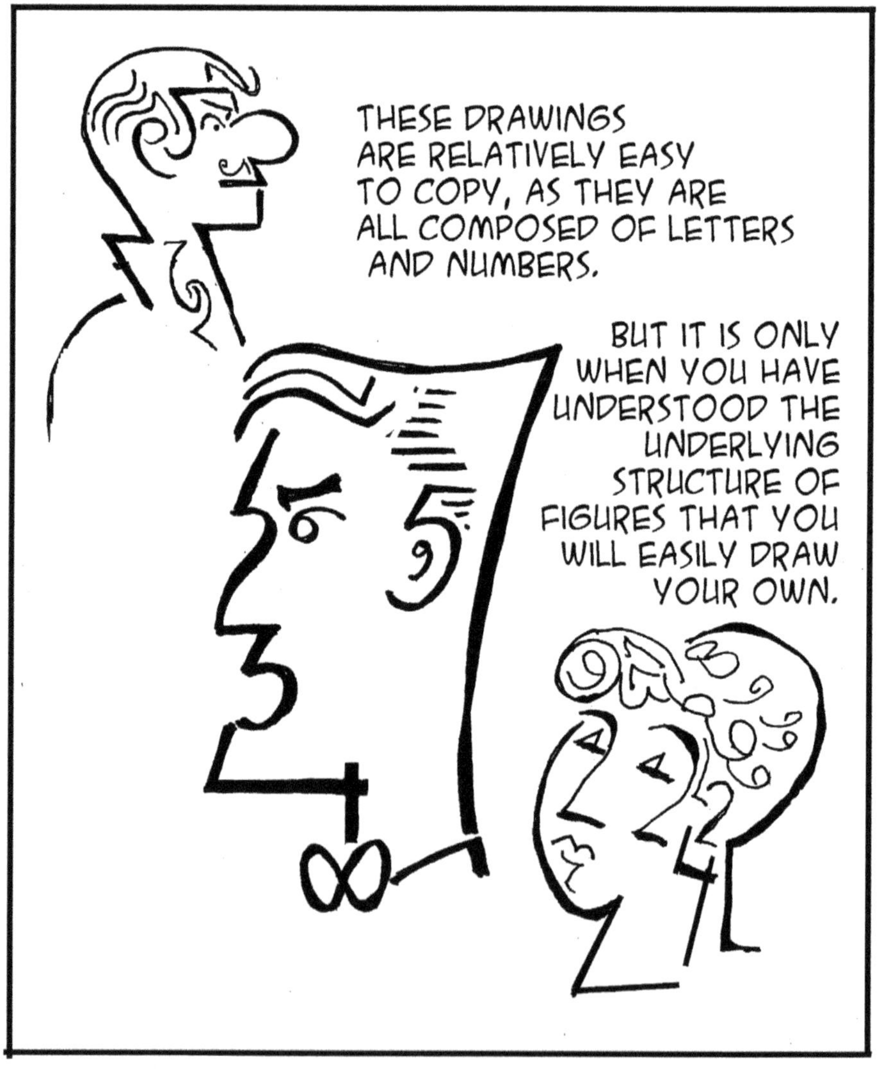

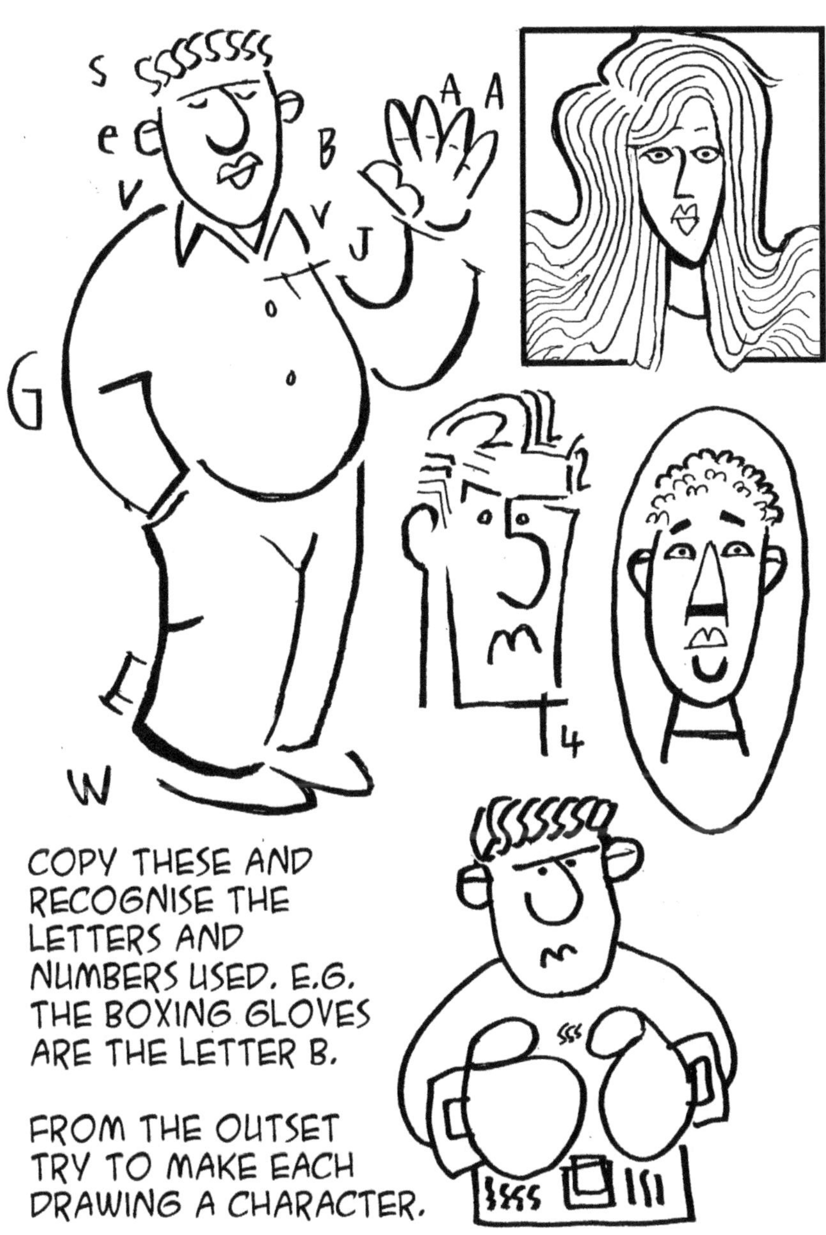
COPY THESE AND
RECOGNISE THE
LETTERS AND
NUMBERS USED. E.G.
THE BOXING GLOVES
ARE THE LETTER B.

FROM THE OUTSET
TRY TO MAKE EACH
DRAWING A CHARACTER.

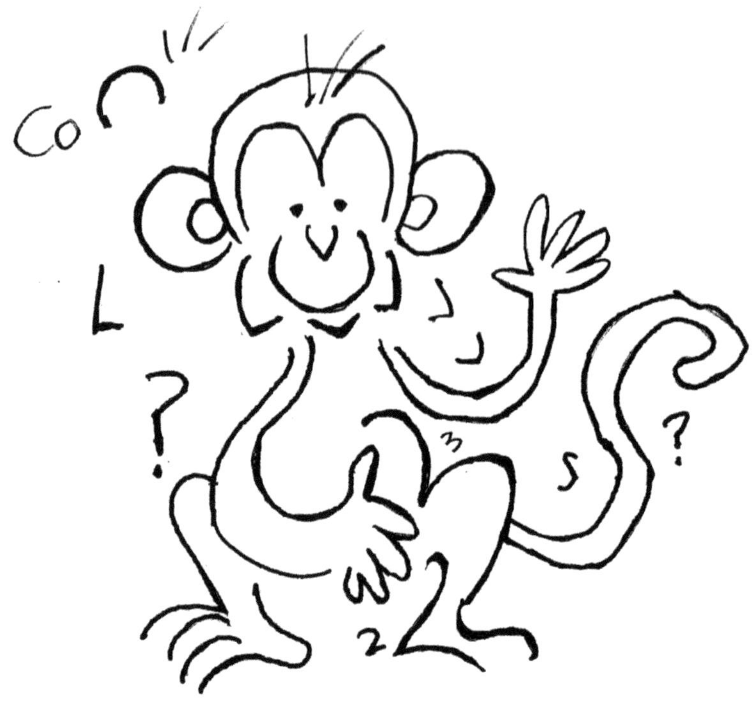

BEFORE YOU COPY THIS DRAWING OF THE MONKEY, FIRST LIST THE LETTERS AND NUMBERSTHAT MAKE IT UP, SO THAT YOU SEE PRECISELY HOW IT WAS CONSTRUCTED

Learn to recognize a letter or number from any point of view. You will find new shapes. Copy everything.

Now that we've incorporated numbers as well as letters, you have twice the number of shapes to use as when you began. Remember, too, that letters look different when they are in capitals or in lower-case letters – they form different shapes.

I want you to look differently at all the shapes of letters, numbers and other writing annotations that you can use without even thinking. Think about the different ways to use them – not to write, but to draw:

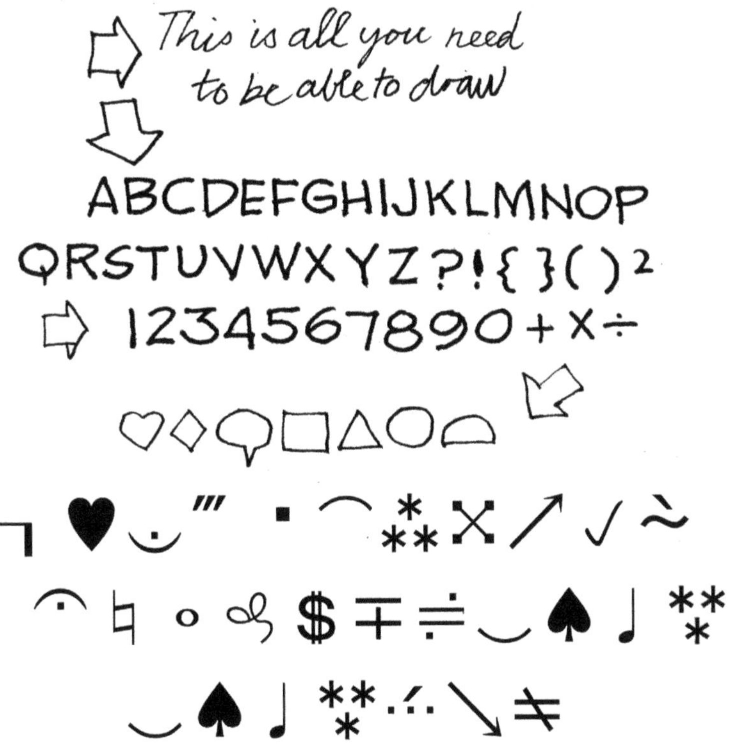

Most of the illustrations you will encounter here are hand-drawn, even rough. At times, lines are not quite parallel or round enough. Drawings, or rather, sketches, are sometimes just rough notes to yourself on the journey to a better life of drawing.

What I have done here is show you some of my own rough drawings. I wanted you to see what an artist's sketchbook looks like, since I believe it will help you on your quest. My sketchbook contains many 'lesser' drawings and lettering that is messy. I hope this encourages you into not feeling intimidated into thinking that a hand-drawn circle has to be perfect, or a line perfectly straight.

Which brings me to the most important lesson I want you to learn from this book: copy everything.

11

COPYCAT

If there's anything I want you to know when you finish this book, it's this: copy other drawings using a pen and paper. That's how you learn to draw. Through imitation.

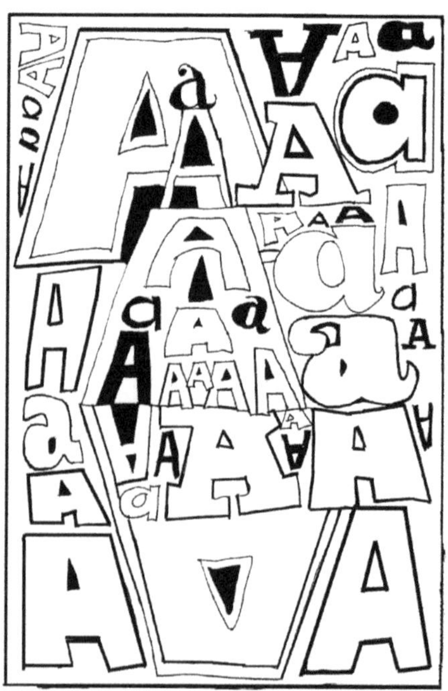

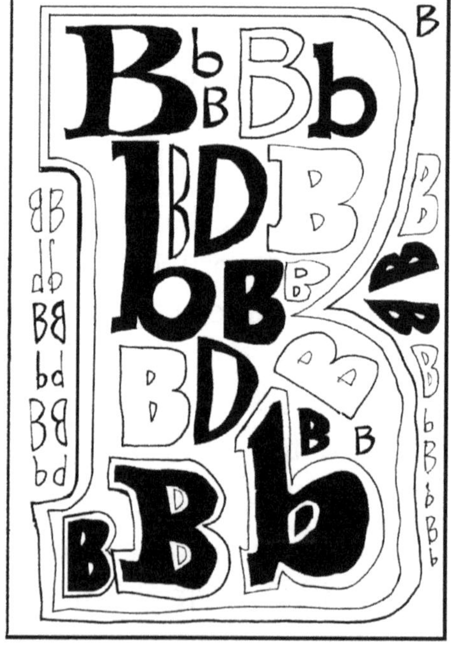

Draw what you see, over and over again. Never be afraid of repetition.

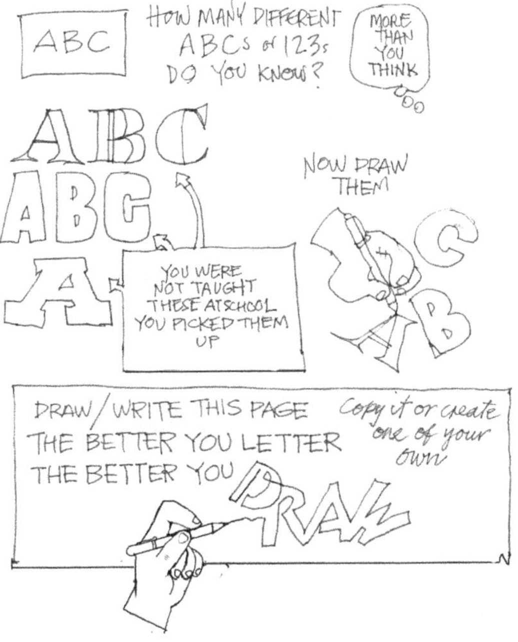

Let us begin with the letter **A** and explore what we can do with that.

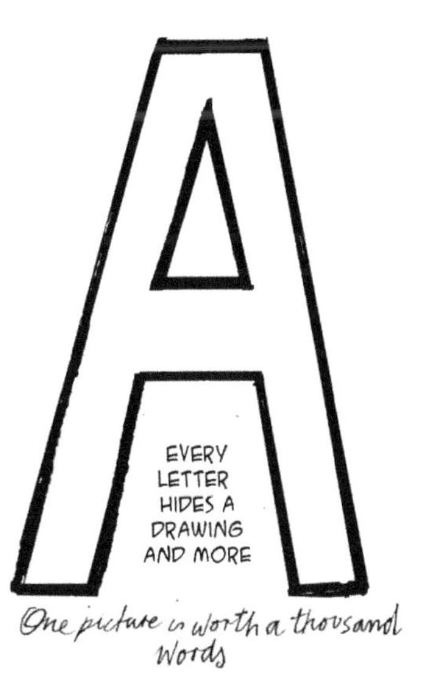

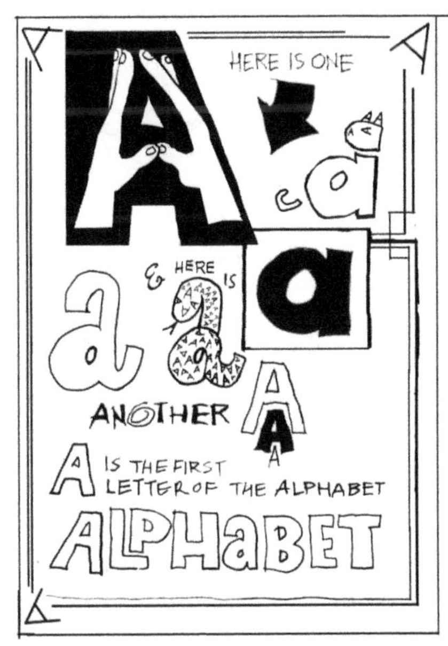

HOW MANY DIFFERENT WAYS CAN YOU DRAW A?

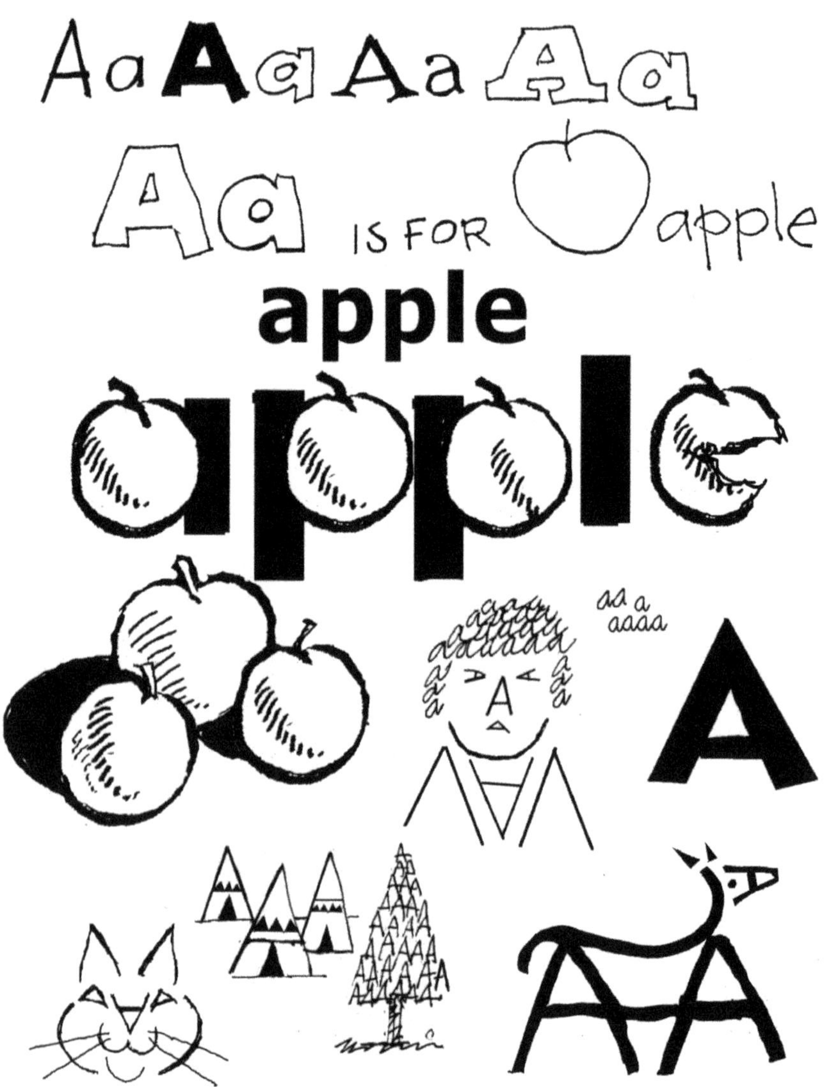

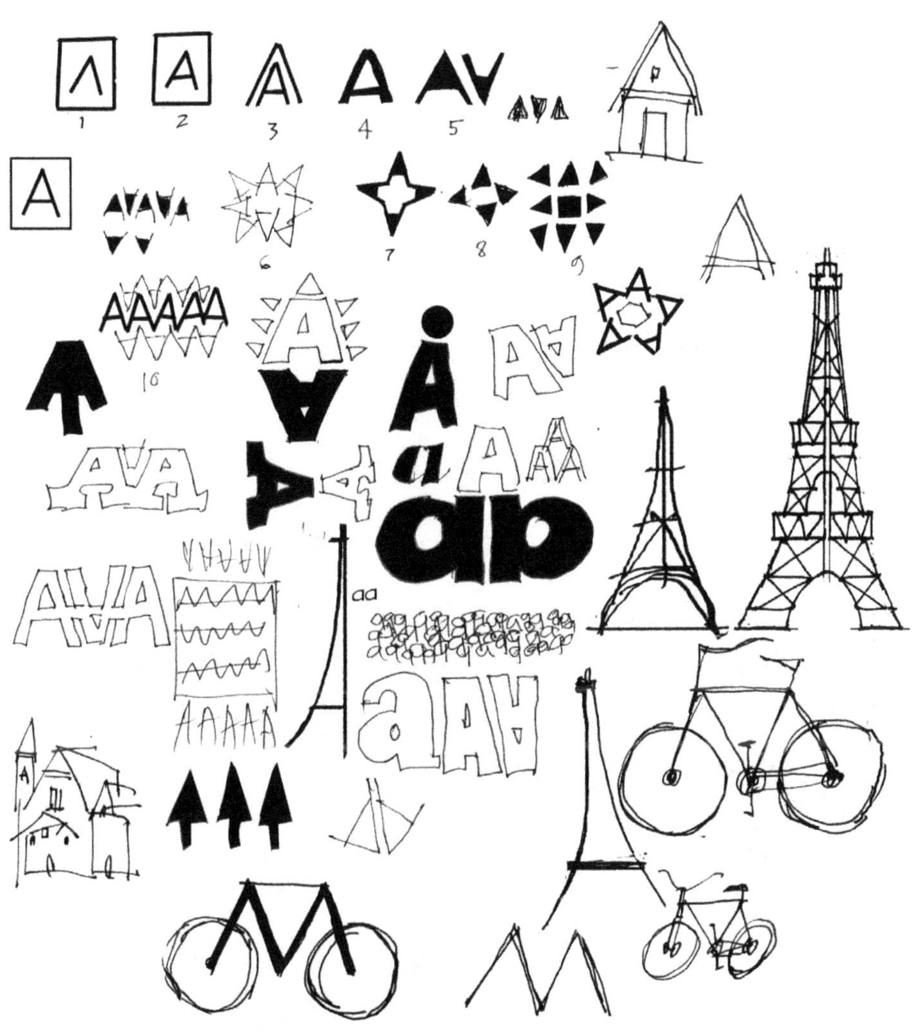

What about the letter **B**?

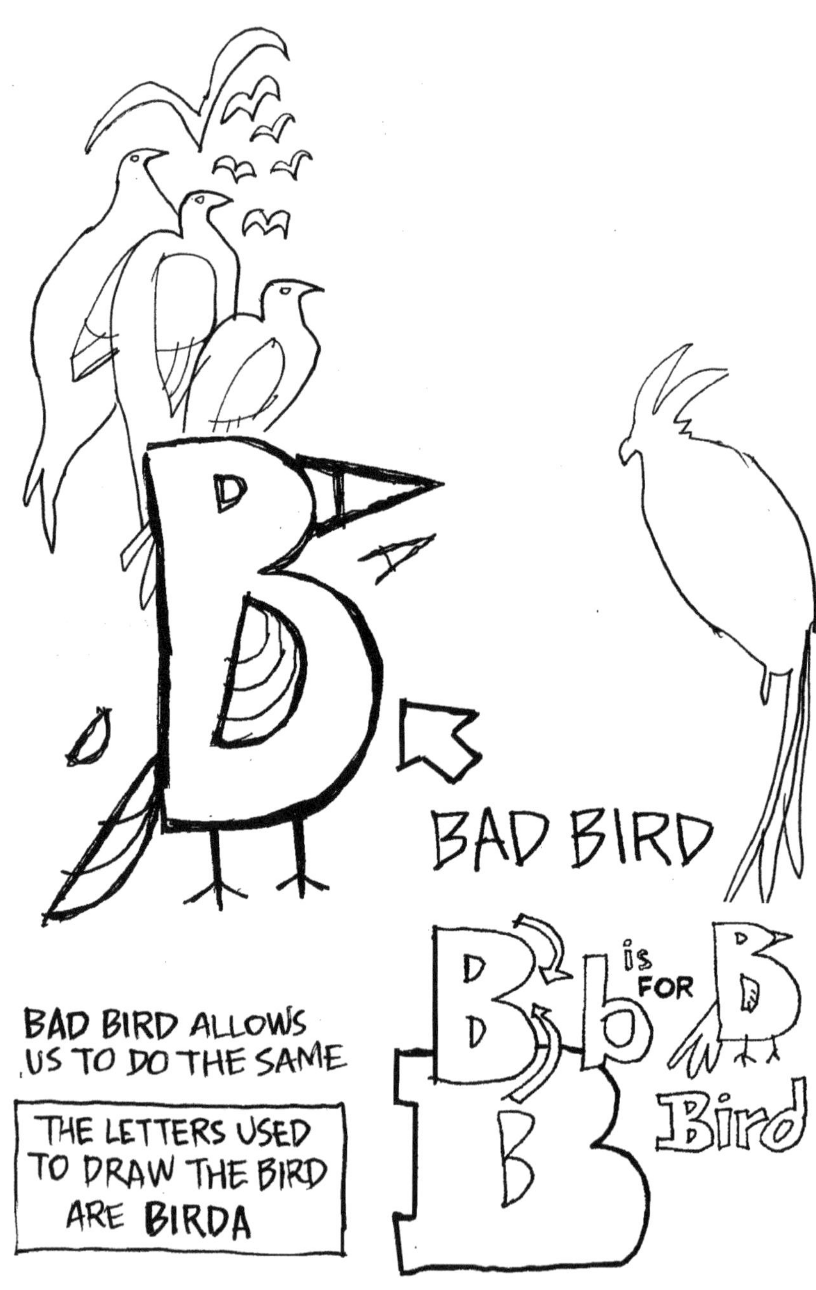

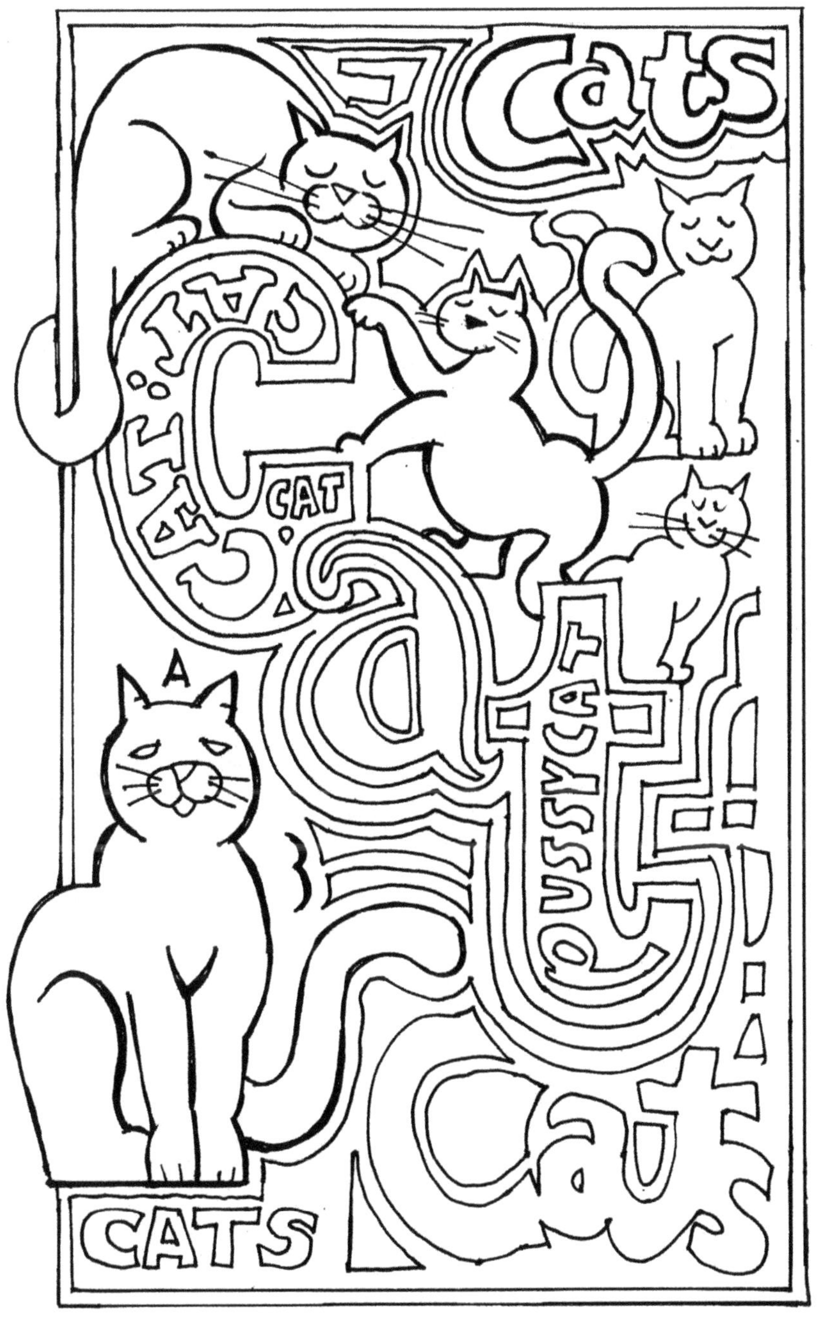
Cats
CAT
CAT
A
PUSSYCAT
CATS
Cats

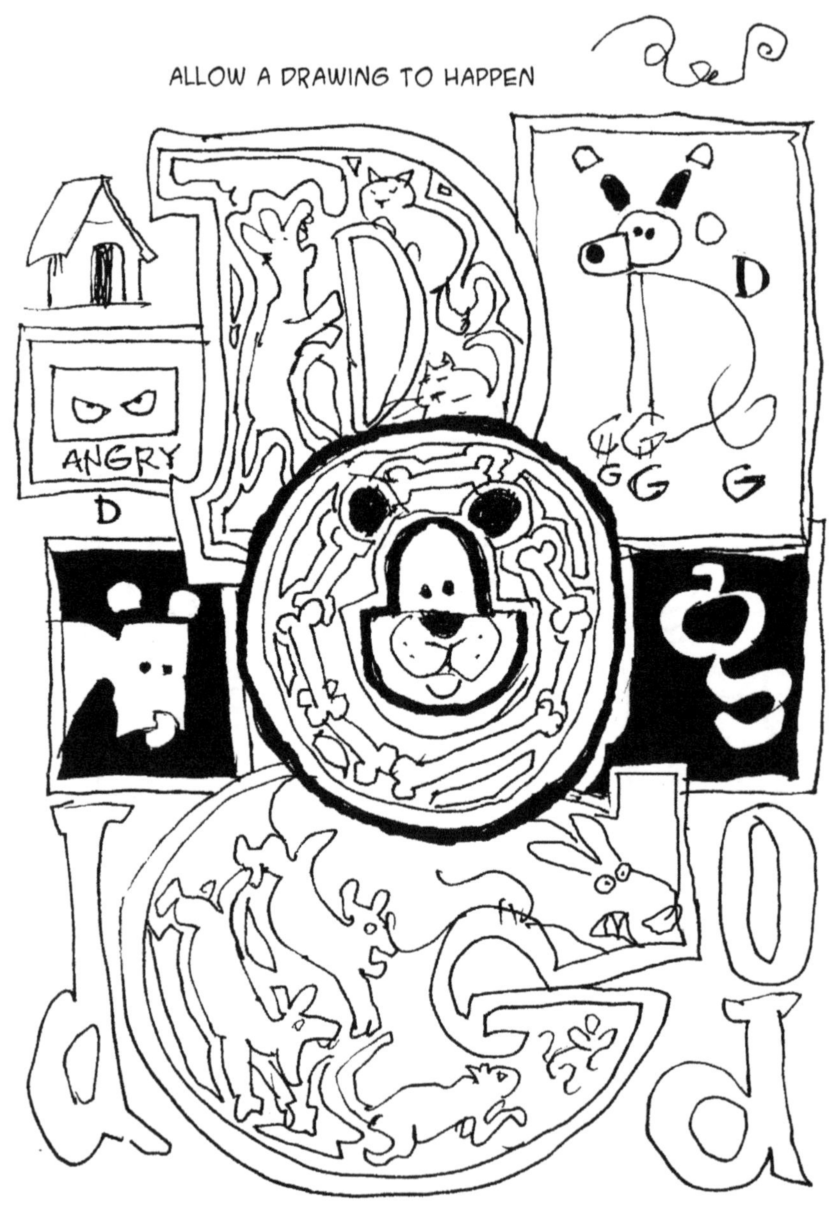
ALLOW A DRAWING TO HAPPEN
ANGRY
D
D
G G G

Let's experiment with **K** and see what we can do.

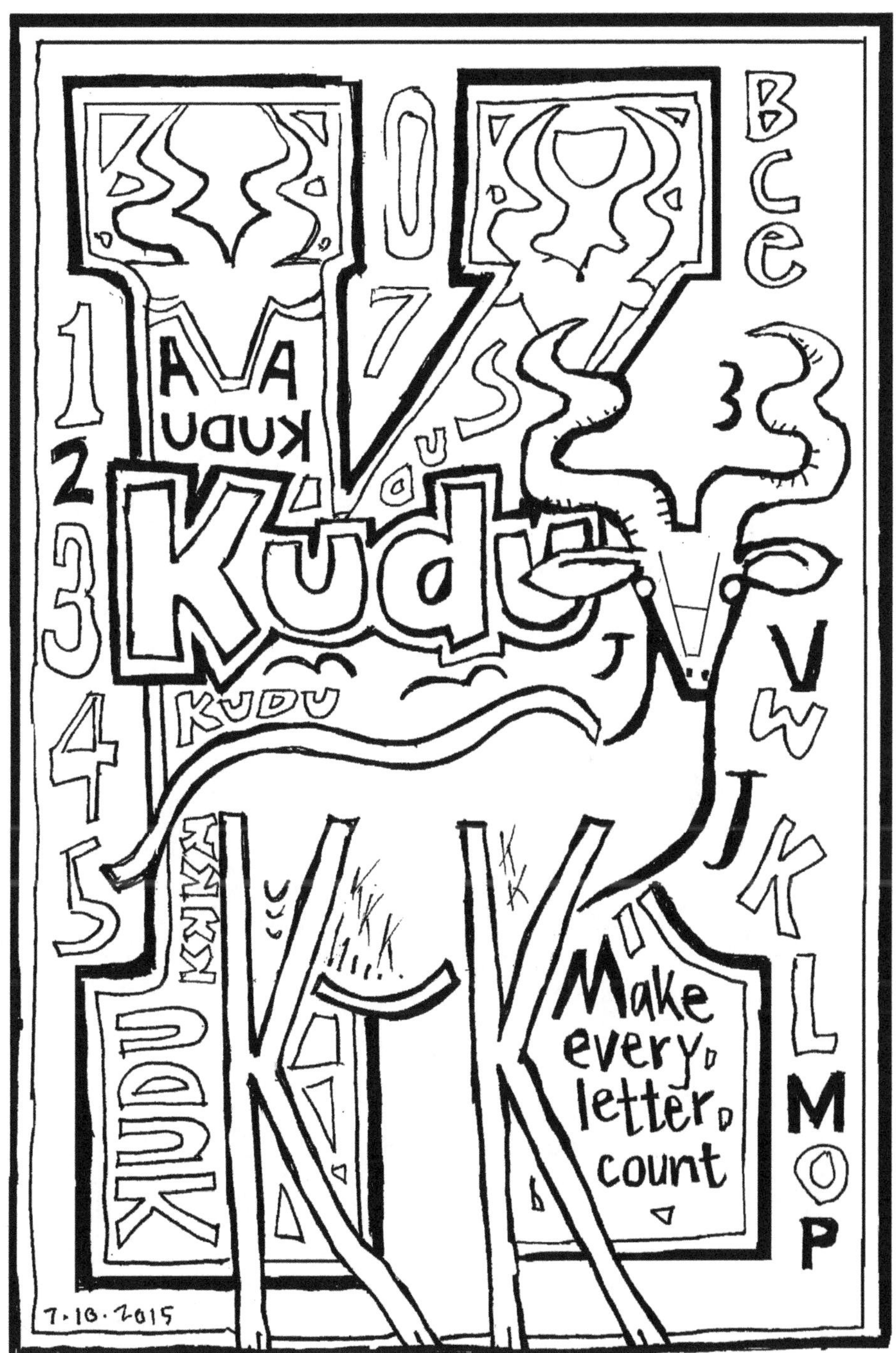

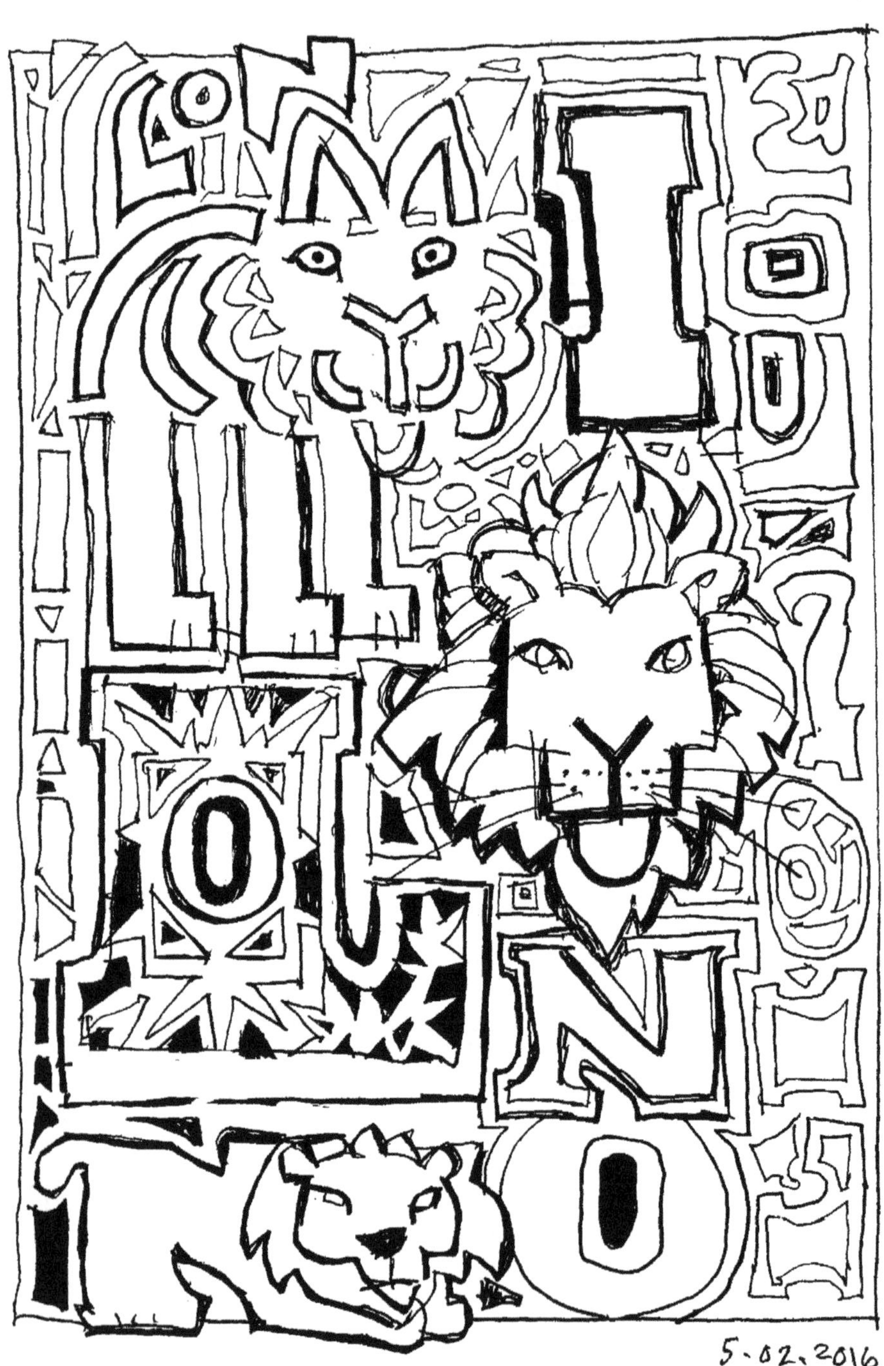
5.02.2016

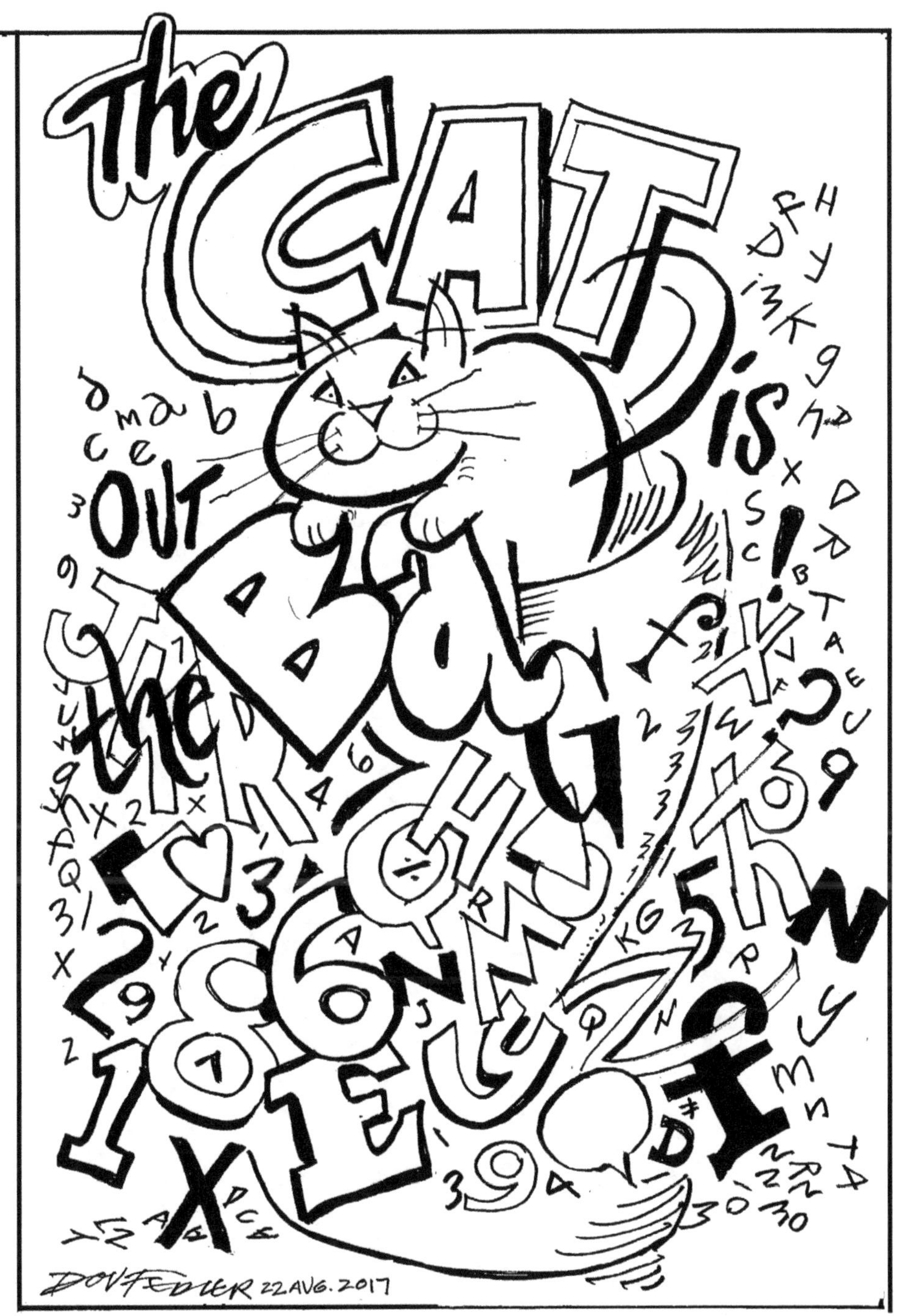
the CAT
is
OUT
the
BAG
DOV FEDLER 22 AUG. 2017

Here are some other shapes for you to have fun with. Can you see them as shapes rather than numbers?

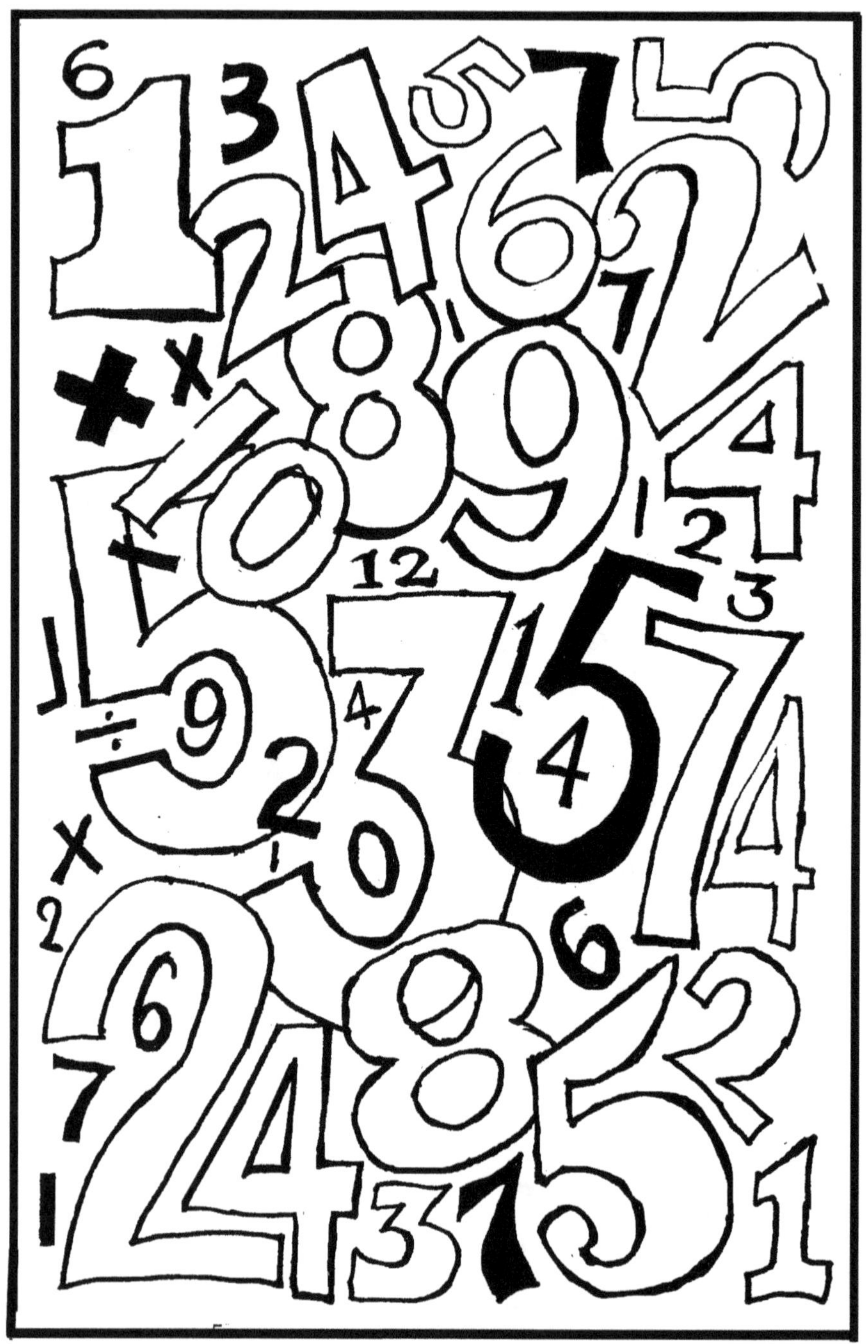

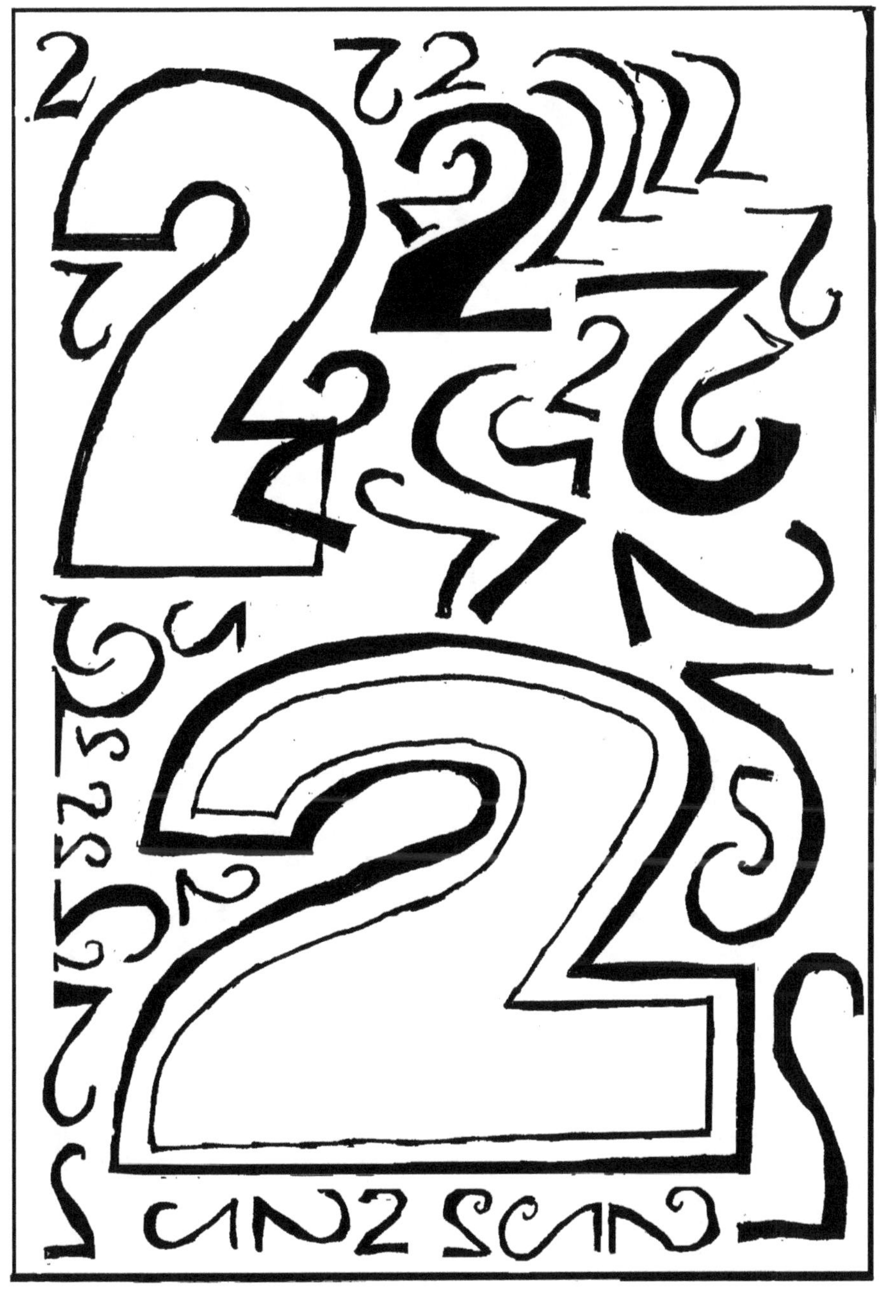

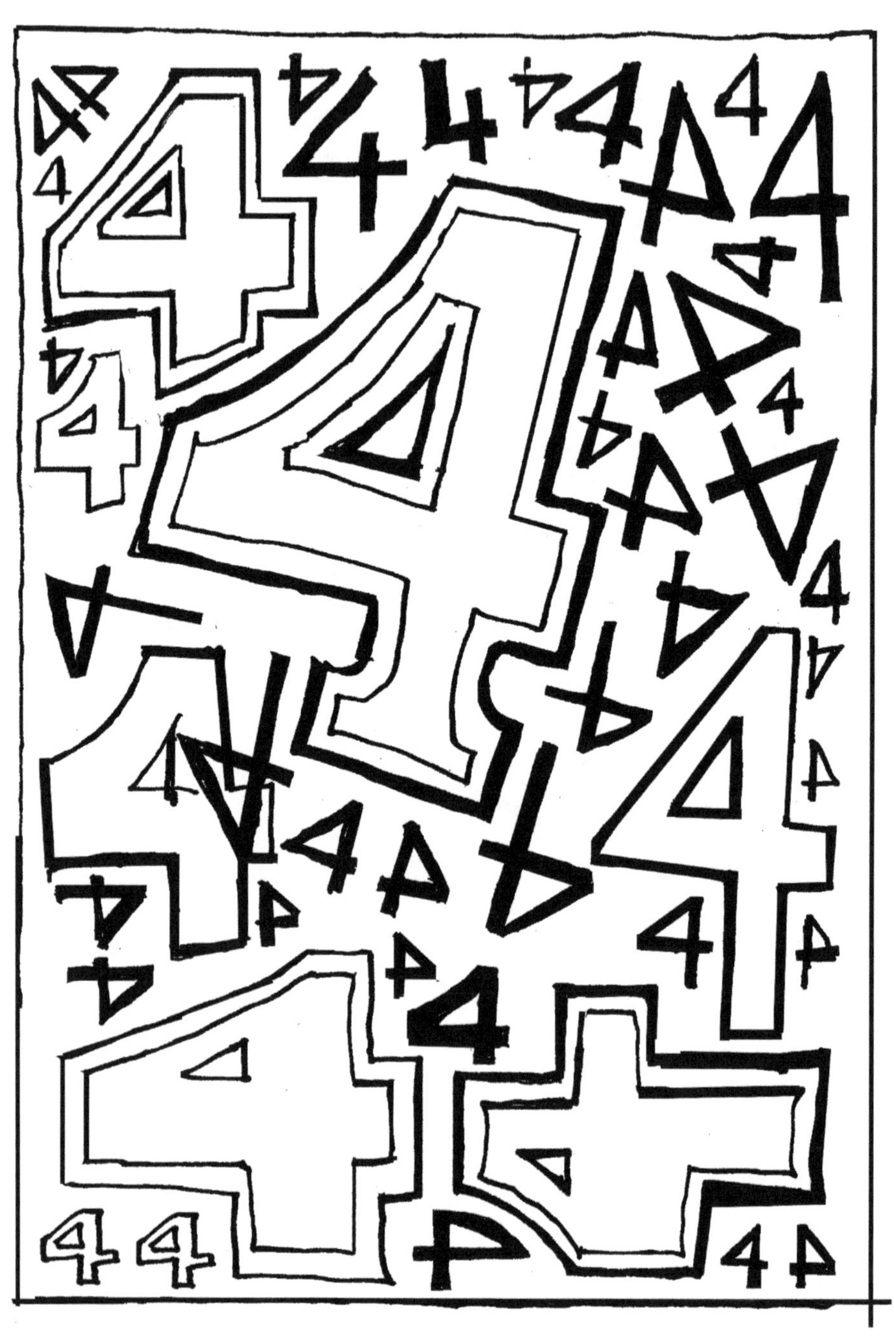

By this stage, you have learnt to recognize these letters and numbers in a myriad of ways. Let's explore how we can play with the shapes of different numbers.

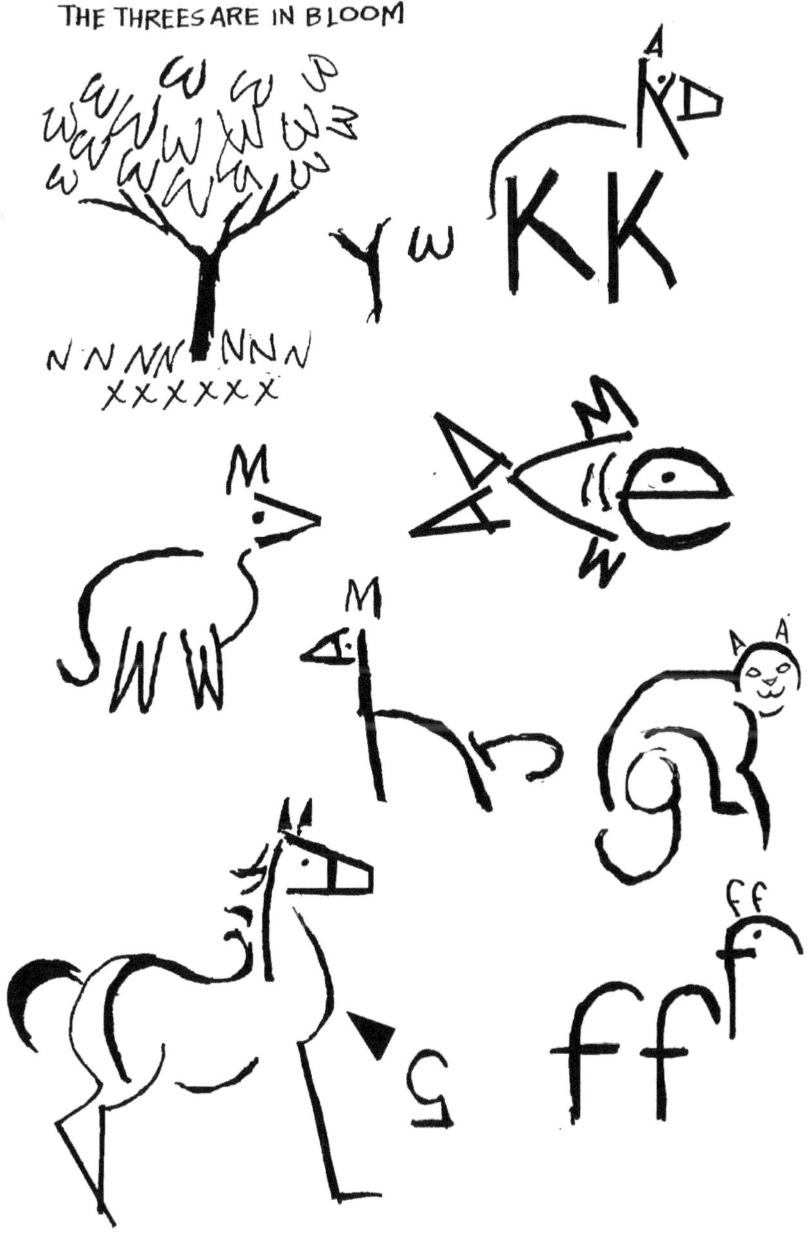

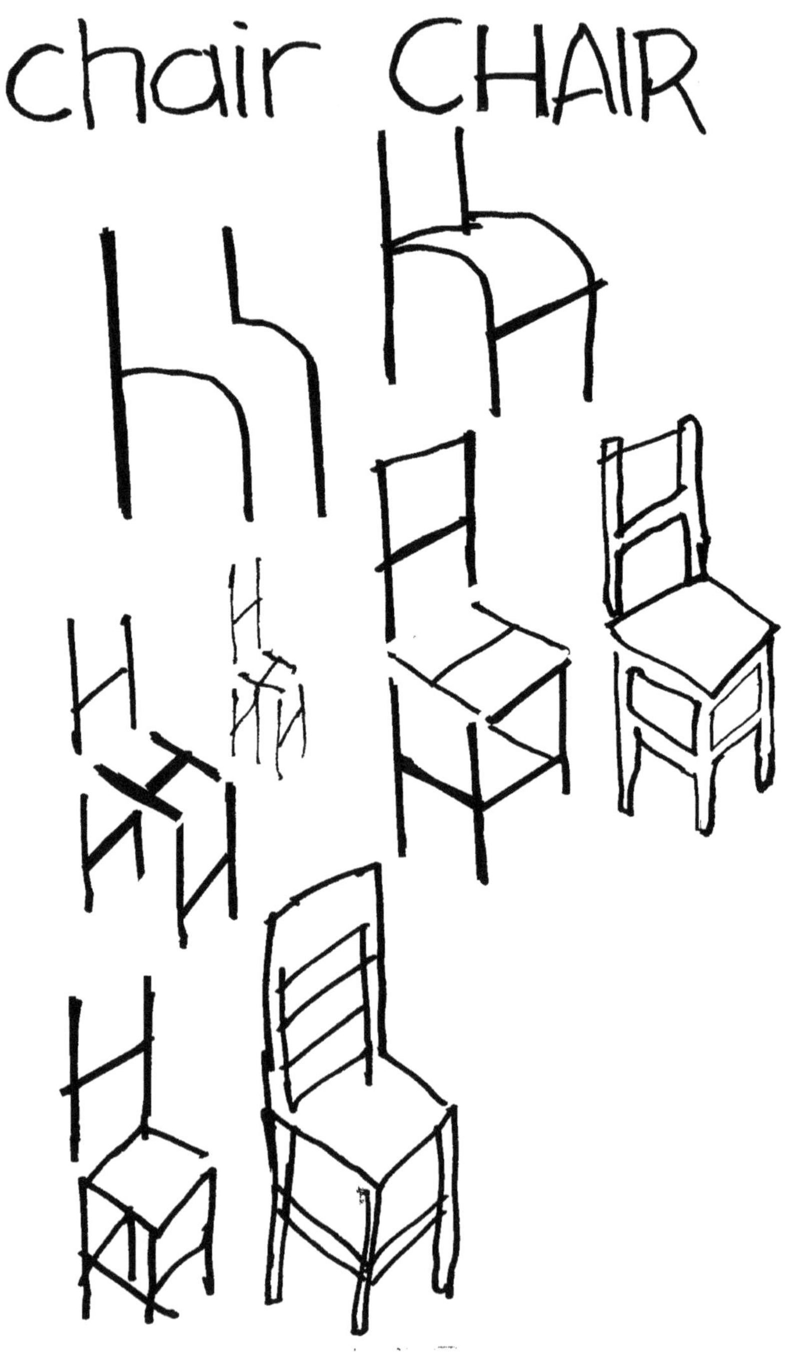
chair CHAIR

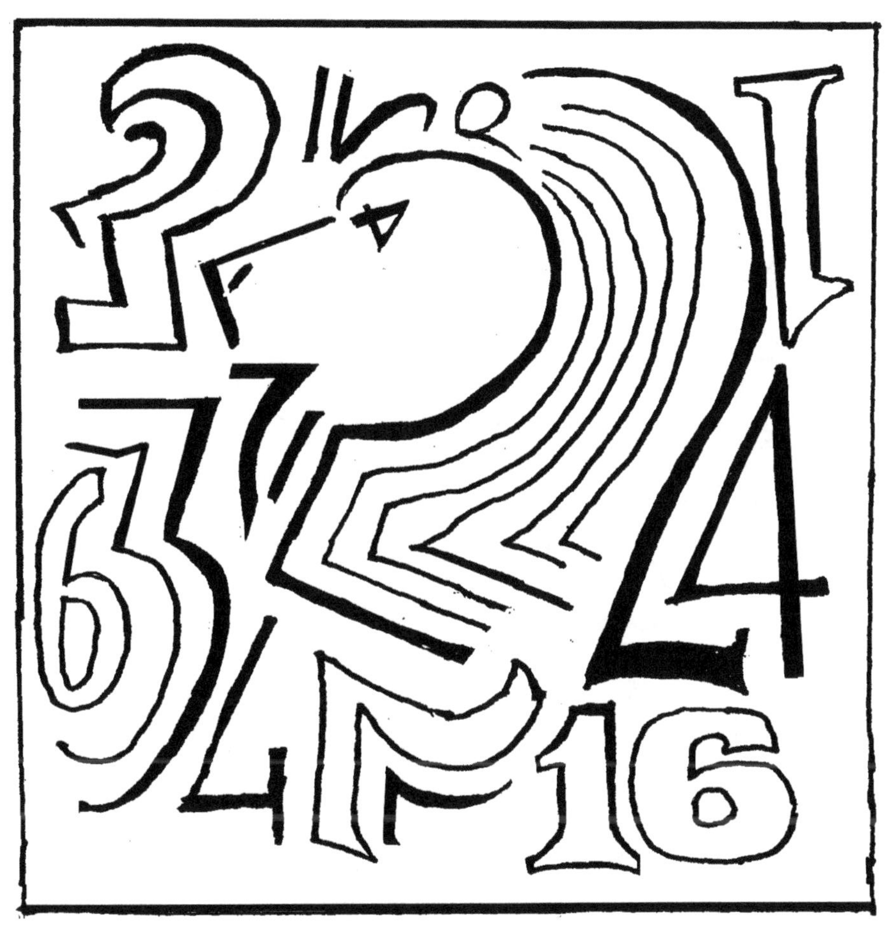

Study and copy these pages of typography and numbers. They demonstrate just how large a vocabulary of drawing you already have. Here is an easy picture to copy using numbers:

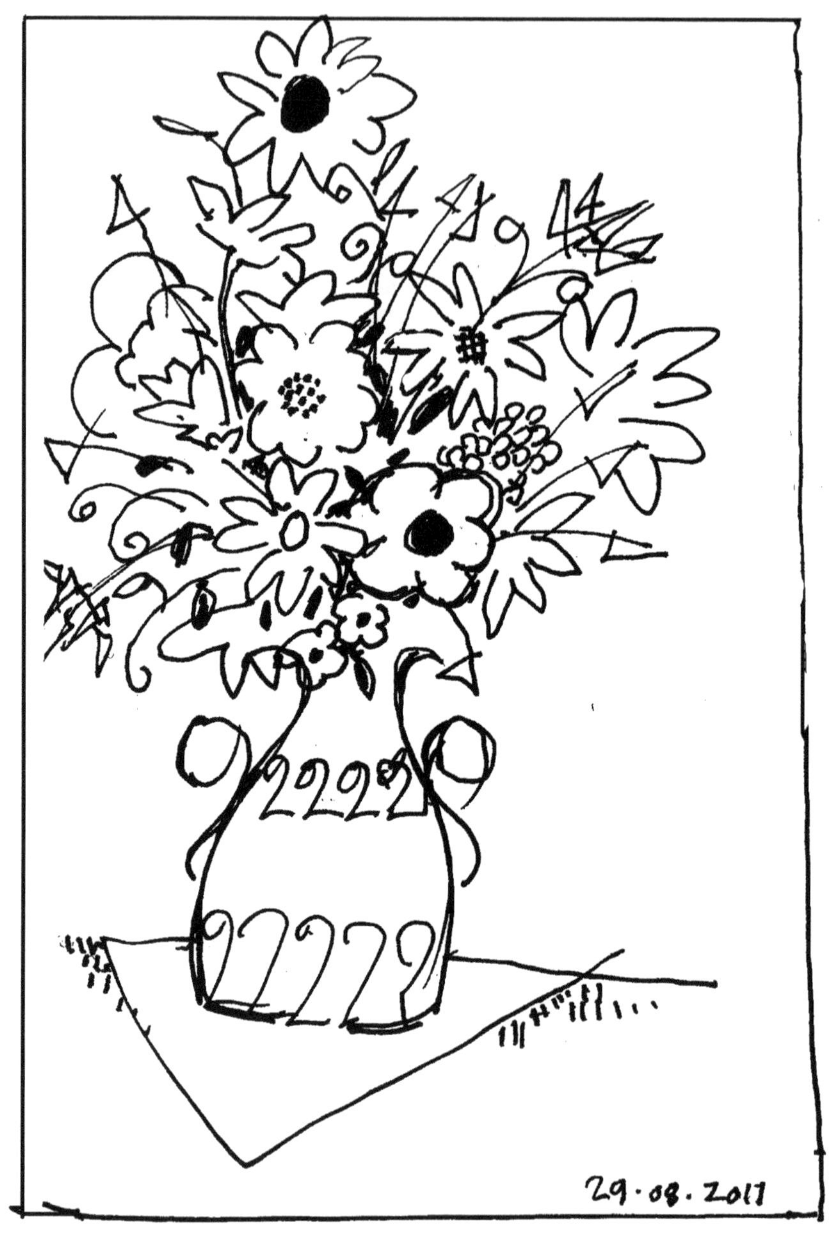

Now look around you at all the objects you'd like to draw. Can you find letters or numbers they resemble in shape?

If so, you're already developing the eye of an artist.

12

YOUR SIGNATURE IS YOUR LOGO

Write your signature – you know, the one you use to sign official forms and cheques. You designed that signature. It is your brand, your personal insignia.

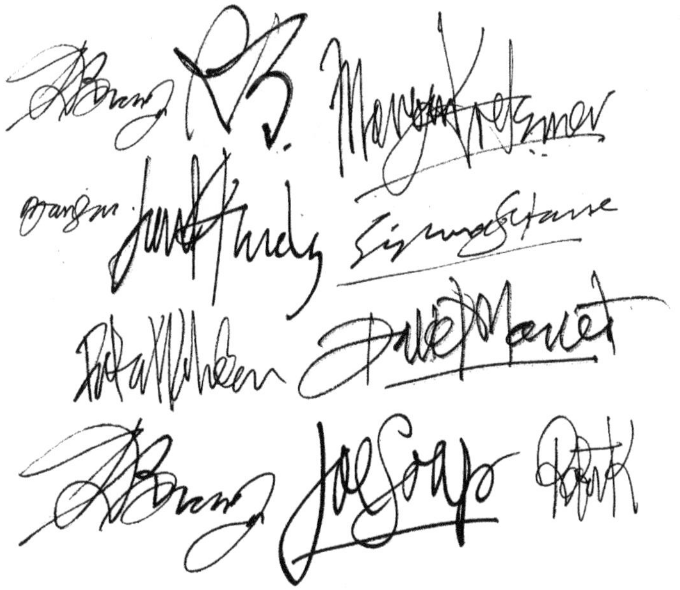

Your signature is a drawing, and we all spend ages designing our signature. So you should – it's your personal logo, your identifying badge.

Your handwriting is unique. Though you may copy, you will draw like no one else. Your signature will stand out. You will make your impression on the world – and that is really all an artist is, whatever the scale. A logo is just an elaboration of this:

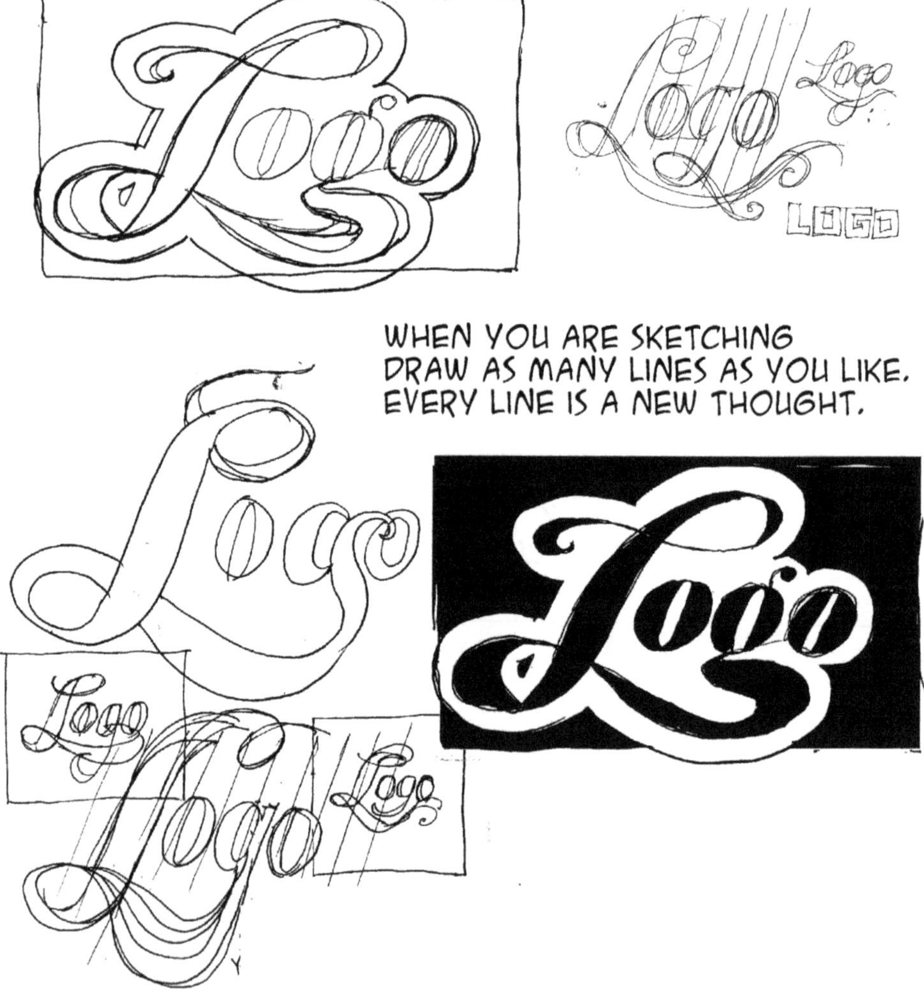

Your signature (or logo) expresses a profound affirmation of yourself – more than that, you have begun to draw like yourself. No one else can draw like you.

Look at all the different logos around you – Nike, Coca-Cola, Walt Disney. Your vocabulary of drawing expands when you can replicate different typefaces. And each one has a different 'feel'. Experiment with different fonts and typefaces until you find the one that fits your personality.

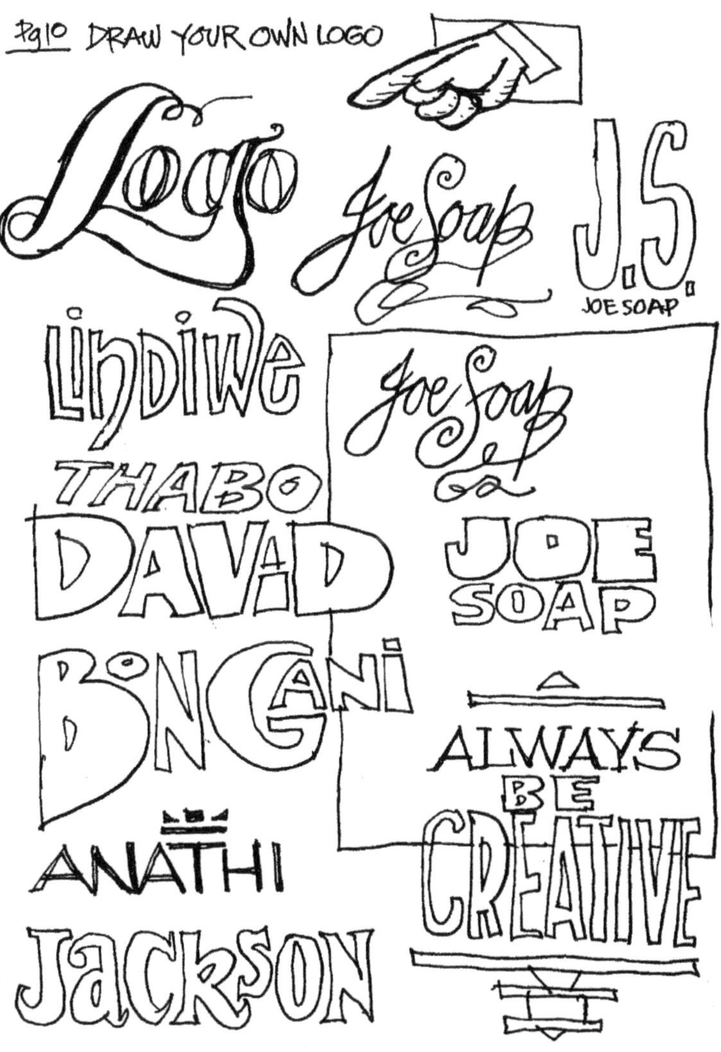

13

THE ABC OF GEOMETRY

Writing evolved from drawing, so we can say that drawing is the origin of written language. Let's look at the Chinese alphabet, which consists of whole images.

The Chinese word for *man* is a single letter that looks like this:

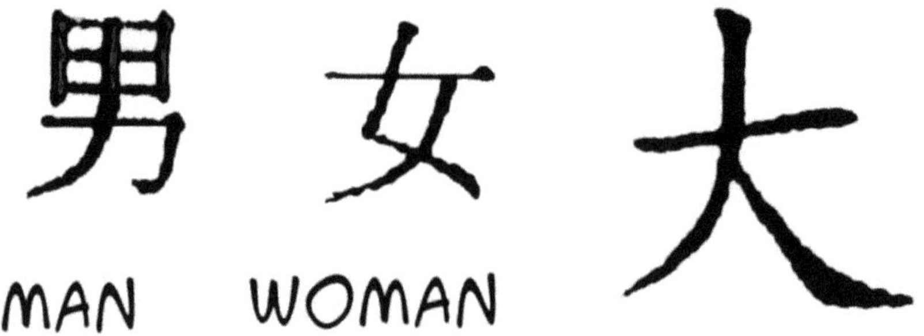

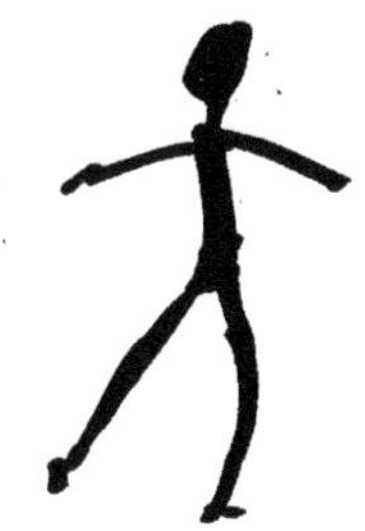

It is easy to see how this progressed from the stick figure above, impressed, perhaps, on a wall in a cave.

Later, in the Roman alphabet (our ABC), letters evolved through simple geometry. Each letter fits within squares or circles.

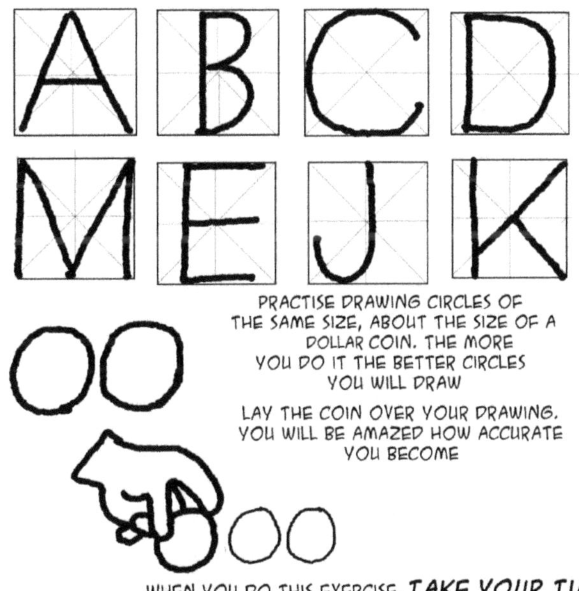

Let's follow the Chinese example by looking at our letters as drawings.

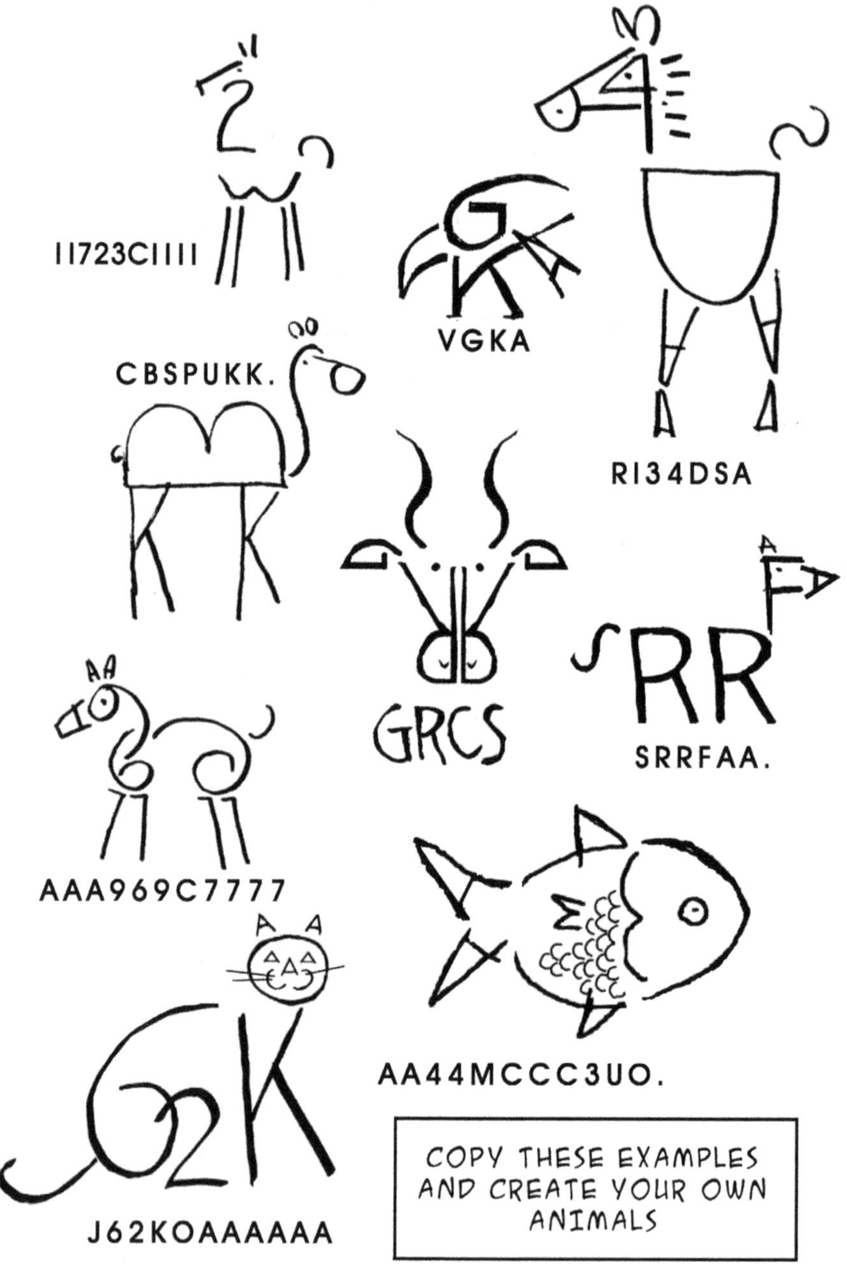

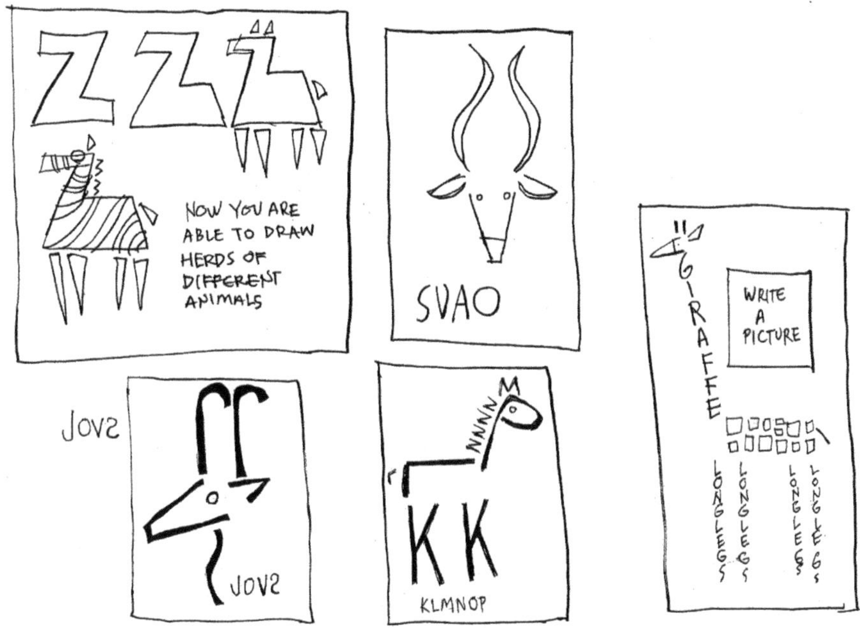

Our remote ancestors were keen observers of the world. They relied on hunting to survive, so they studied their prey the way an art student studies a model. San paintings of people greatly resemble the Chinese character for *man*. Their pictures are maps and signposts. Hunting was crucial to existence, so they learnt to paint accurate depictions about which animals grazed in a particular area – and even showed how they should be hunted. Other members of their families would then know how to follow the signs.

These images are masterful in color, detail and effect.

In this manner, writing and drawing crossed over at inception.

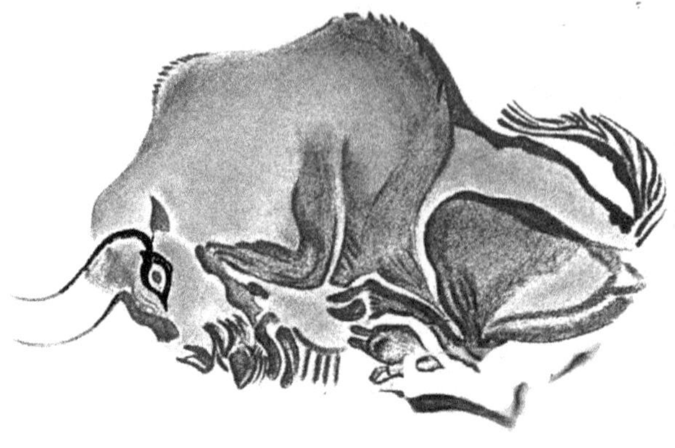

Now let’s examine their artistic genius more closely:

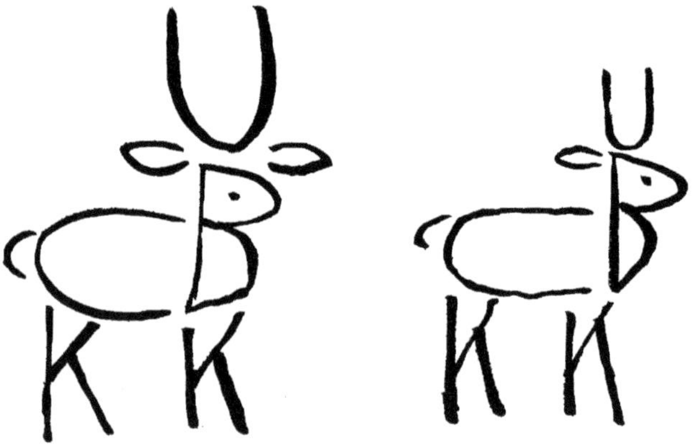

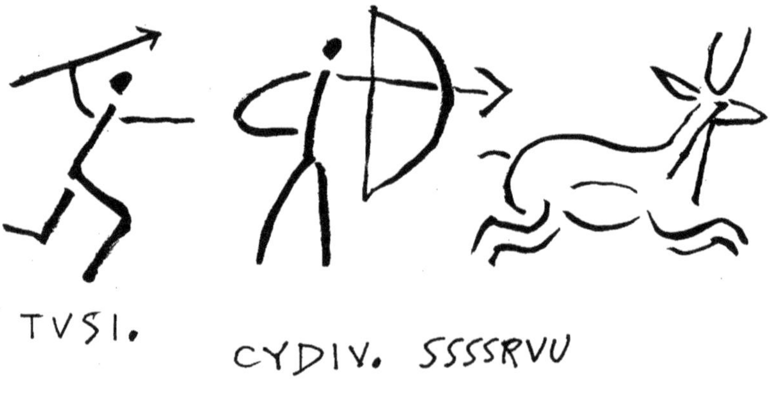

TVSI.

CYDIV. SSSSRVU

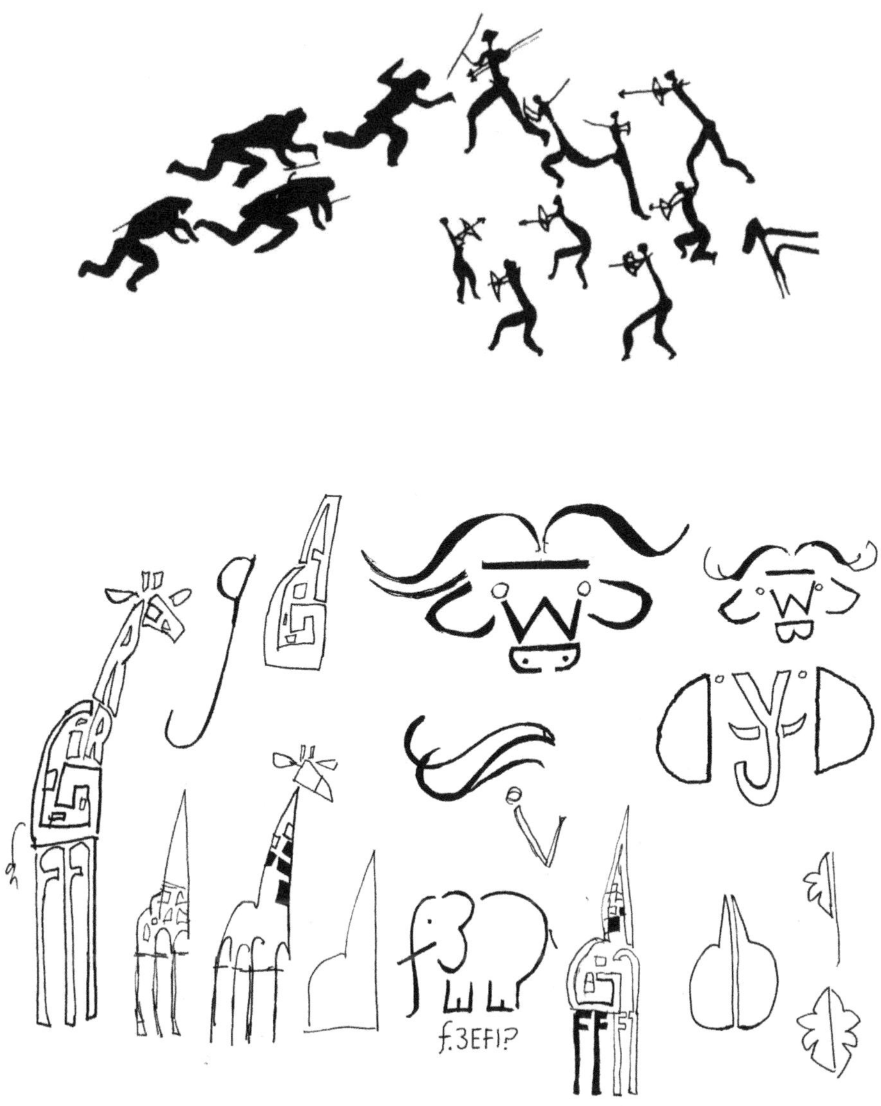

Consider the next drawing – that of a buck. Try and draw it. Begin at the top with its horns. Then draw the head and neck, using both letters and numbers. Treat every letter and number as a component of the drawing, as if they all belong together.

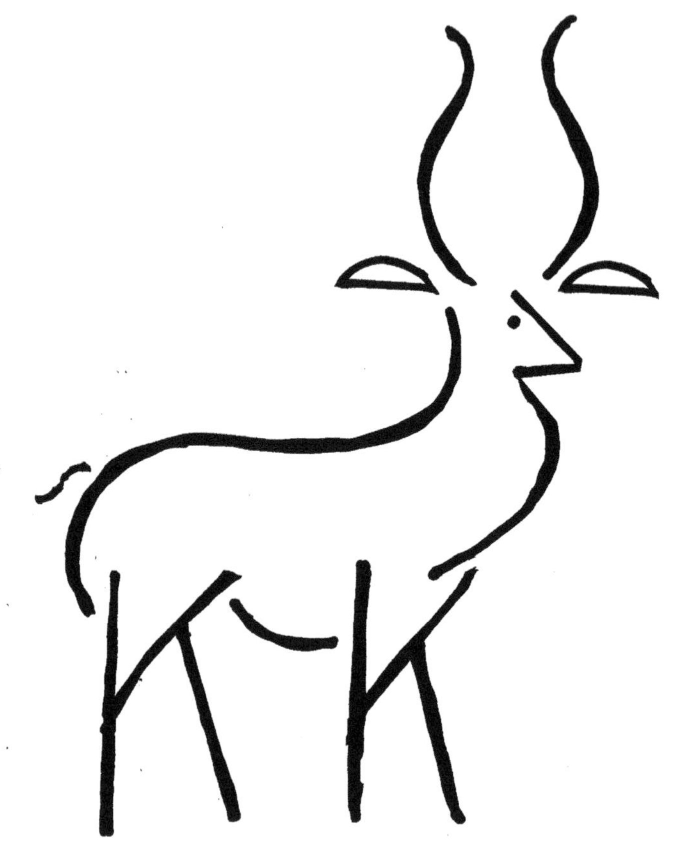

An object is spelt out by different shapes, or letters. You could call this the alphabet of geometry – one you need to master. In many ways, this is easier to grasp than the alphabet of words (in English, anyway).

In the drawing of the buck, I've used the number 3 among the letters.

Compare San paintings with the signs (our signs!) below, intended to communicate basic information. Who comes first? The instinct to mark these directions is the same. To the prey – or the loo.

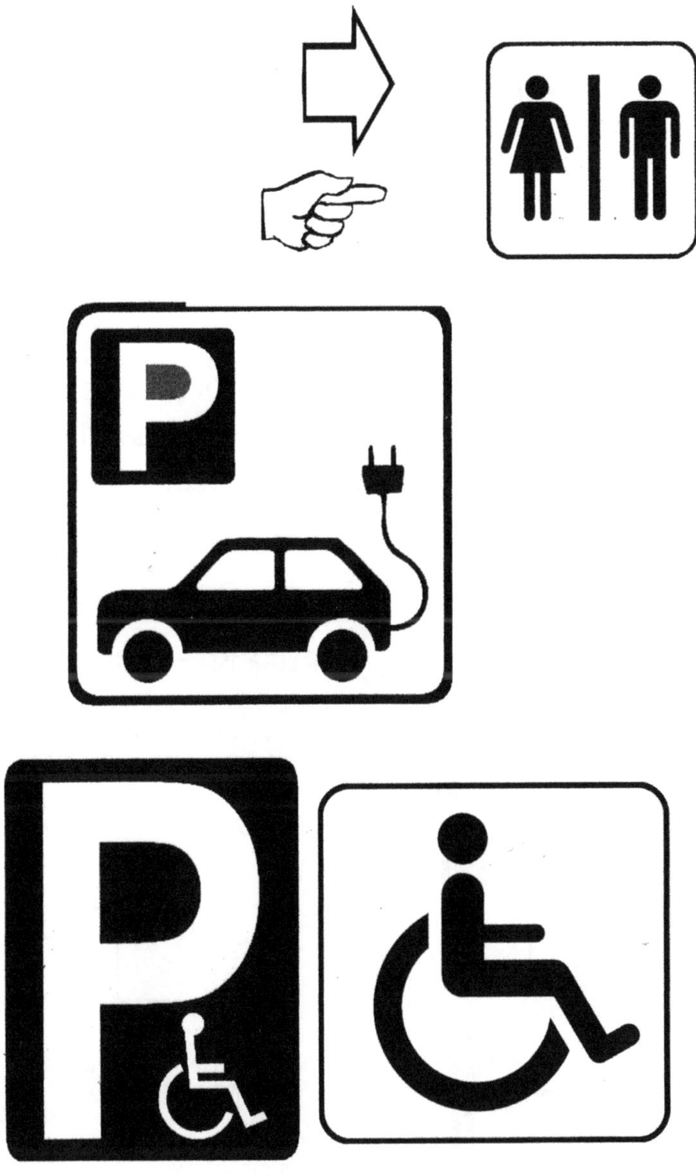

14

MIRROR, MIRROR

Now that you've got the basics, it's time to double up. I want you to stand up and put your hands above your head. Now make circles with them, bring them down, then across, as if you were conducting an orchestra or guiding a plane into its parking space.

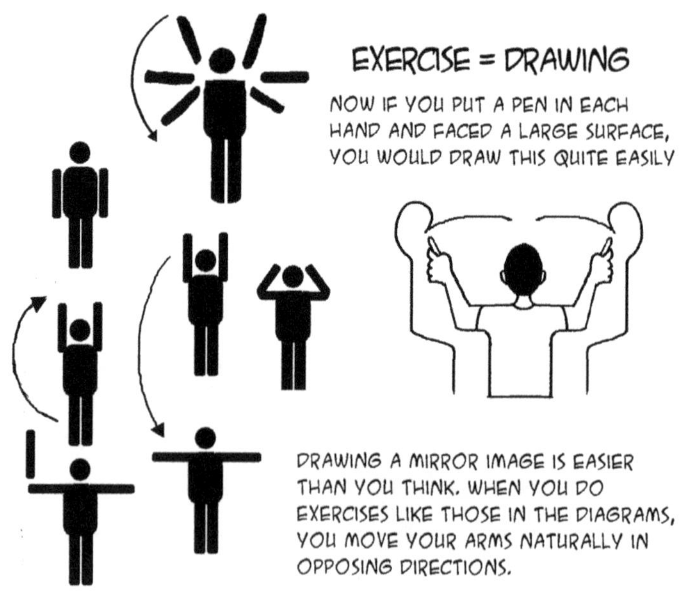

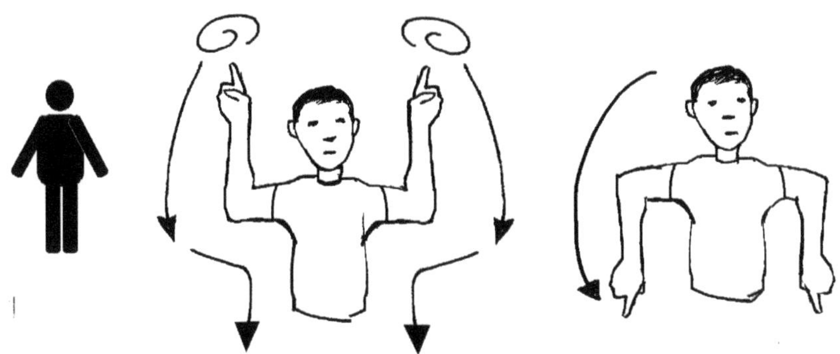

Now imagine the exercise with a pen in each hand facing a board. Instead of exercising, you're drawing with both your right and left hands.

Guess what? You've just begun to draw a lion's face.

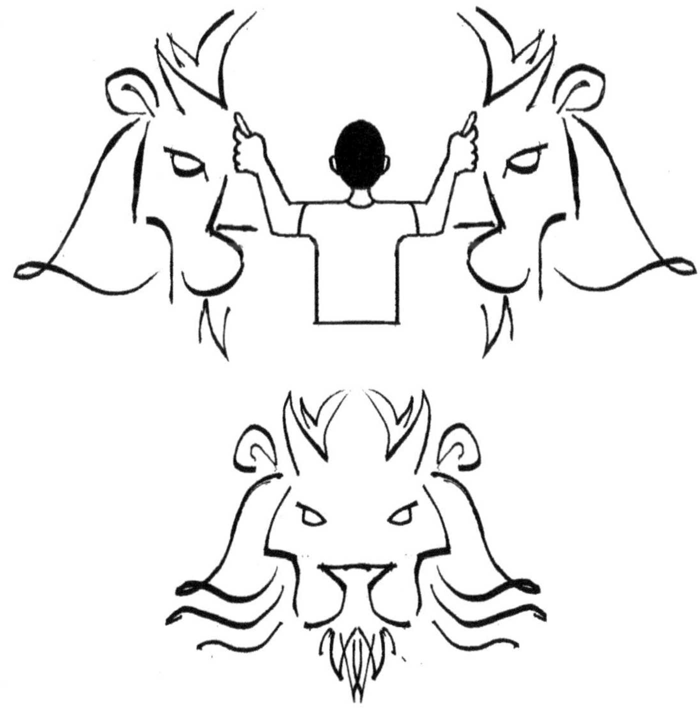

Most creatures are symmetrical when cut down the middle, so what you draw on the one side needs simply to be mirrored on the other. Learn to see these characters in mirror image, or upside down.

If you are right-hand dominant, try to draw with your left hand, and vice versa. Drawing in mirror image also breaks the boundary of defining a letter as one thing. Practise drawing letters from all angles, and patterns will present themselves.

The beauty of nature is that it is based on symmetry. So instead of thinking about *anatomy*, which sounds difficult and medical (not to mention serious), we're going to think in terms of 'architecture' or 'form'. In order for us to draw something, we want to understand its design and construction – how it works.

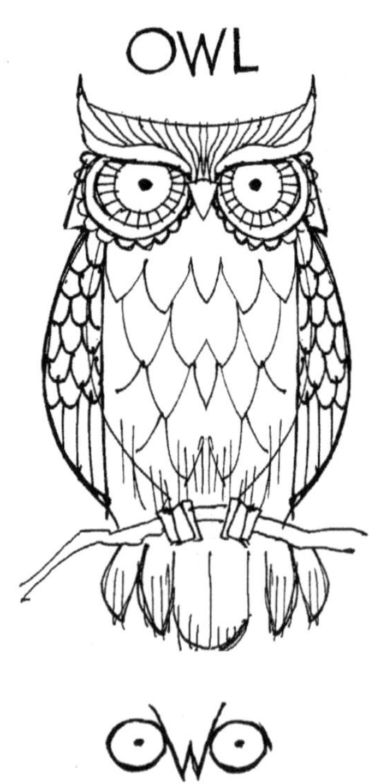

15

KNOWING HOW THINGS WORK HELPS US TO DRAW THEM

If you really want to draw something, you need to understand how it works.

Think about it in terms of a building. Building construction sets out, in the form of a plan, how the structure should be engineered. This is how we need to think about anything we attempt to draw.

A building begins with a site, the location on which it will be erected. Once the site has been measured and understood, the architect will begin to plot what goes where. The architect will then draw it in three dimensions and will often build a model of the design. This is to ensure that everyone understands how the building functions – based on its intended purpose, location and the needs it must meet, both aesthetically and practically.

The following are some examples of plans dating back to Roman and Gothic (twelfth century) times.

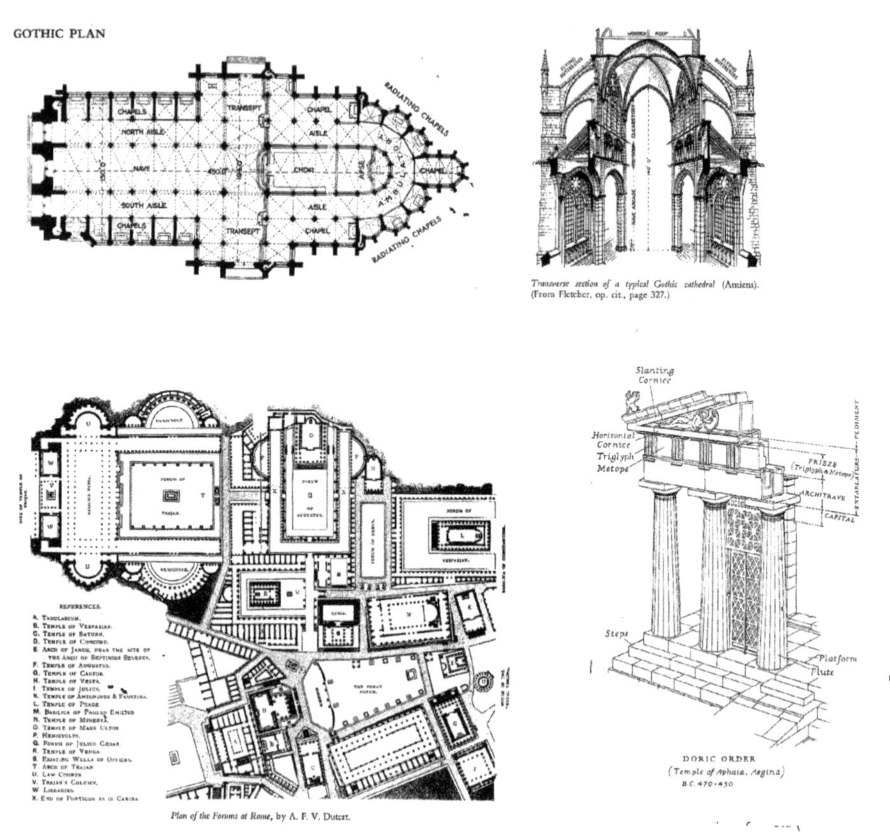

Transverse section of a typical Gothic cathedral (Amiens). (From Fletcher, op. cit., page 327.)

Plan of the Forums at Rome, by A. F. V. Dutert.

When we draw, we too should begin with a plan. Plans often take the form of rough sketches. In the rough sketch, we begin to explore the mechanics of what we are drawing.

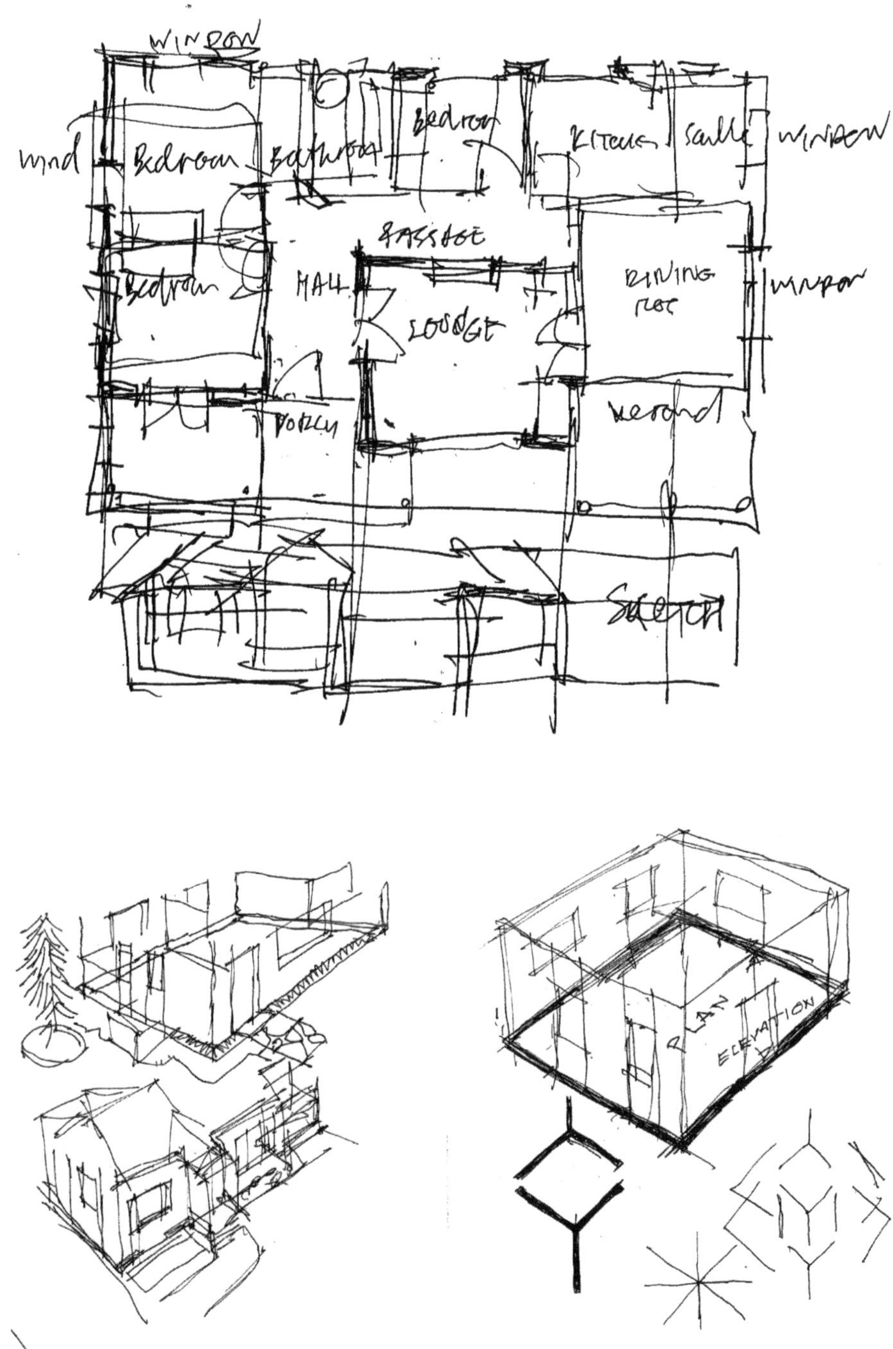
WINDOW
Bedroom
Bedroom
Bedroom
HALL
LOUNGE
PORCH
WINDOW
SKETCH
PLAN
ELEVATION

This allows us to plan and think ahead about all the elements of our picture. So we begin to conceive of constructing it architecturally so that all the parts work, in the same way as a building must work – functionally, aesthetically and logistically.

Seeing an object is just a part of observing it. Watching a horse gallop is a beautiful sight, but understanding how its body parts unite in that action enlarges the picture. Observing how a cat stalks is an exercise in understanding the difference in physical function between it and a horse. A horse cannot crouch, though. Broadly, its body parts are in many ways similar to those of a cat, a hunting animal with its colours and markings serving as camouflage.

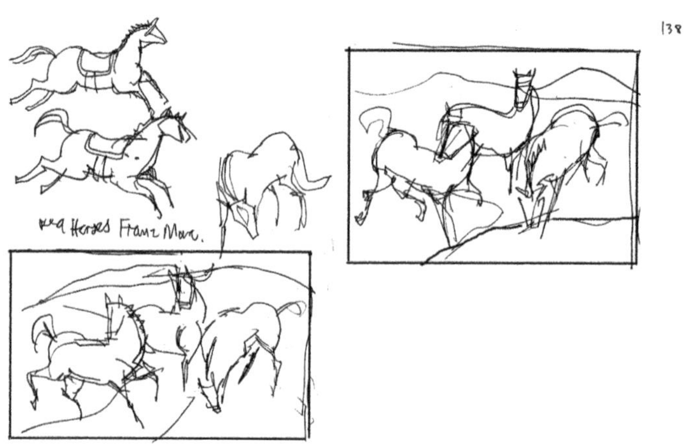

Here is a quick exercise to test your observation. Without consulting Google, draw a bicycle.

All you need to draw is a diagram, not an artistic rendition. Now imagine you are teaching a class that has never seen a bicycle. They have no idea what a bicycle is. For you to draw it, you must understand how a bicycle works – you must understand its function and architecture.

Try drawing a watering can alongside a bicycle.

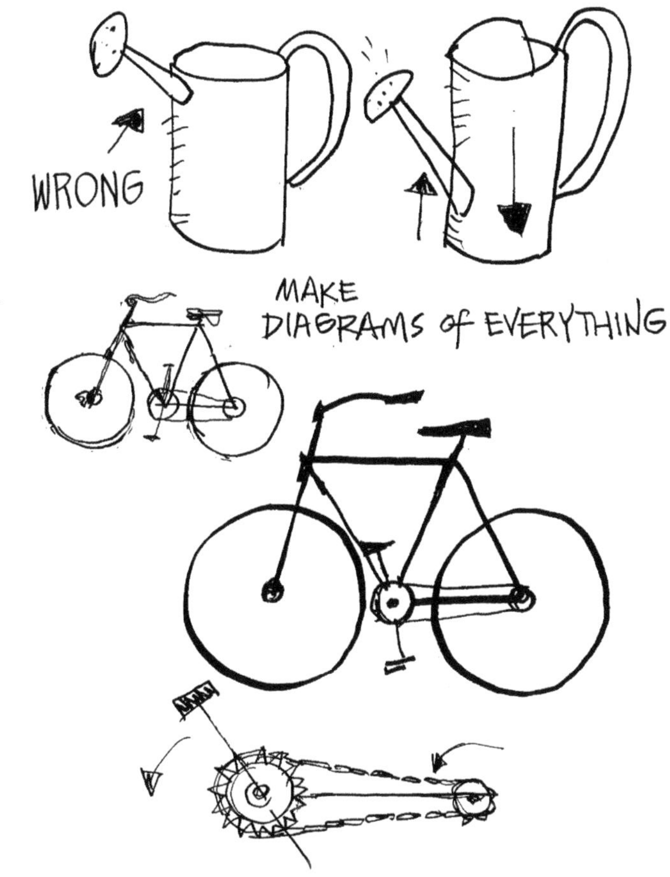

The reason why we can't draw these things is because we haven't thought these objects through. The principles of a watering can are based on physics. The spout must begin at the bottom so that the weight of water in the container forces the water up. An old-fashioned teapot is constructed on the same principles. If you drew the watering can with its spout coming out at the top, you have failed to understand the simplicity of it. The weight of the water at the top is what drives the water down – and up the spout.

To work, a bicycle depends on simple geometry. Its frame is triangulated – one of the strongest methods of construction: the weight is evenly distributed. The bike is propelled by the movement of the back wheel, powered by the pedals, which drive a cogged wheel chain-linked to the back one.

The genius of the design is that the front wheel is free to turn the vehicle. Its invention changed the world of transport. It began as a drawing.

Both of these examples – the watering can and the bicycle – highlight the differences in observing and seeing. To observe properly, we must think, though many of us have given up that old-fashioned pastime. I'd like to see it revived. Our world needs better thinkers to help solve the problems we've created without thinking.

16

FLOWERS AND FACES

Perhaps you don't feel ready to tackle a complex drawing. So let's begin with a vase of flowers. Both vase and flowers are unthreatening and uncomplicated structures. A clay vase is turned to shape it on a potter's wheel. Flowers grow in strict geometrical patterns in a similar circular way.

Study this drawing – and then draw a vase of flowers of your own without referring to the example.

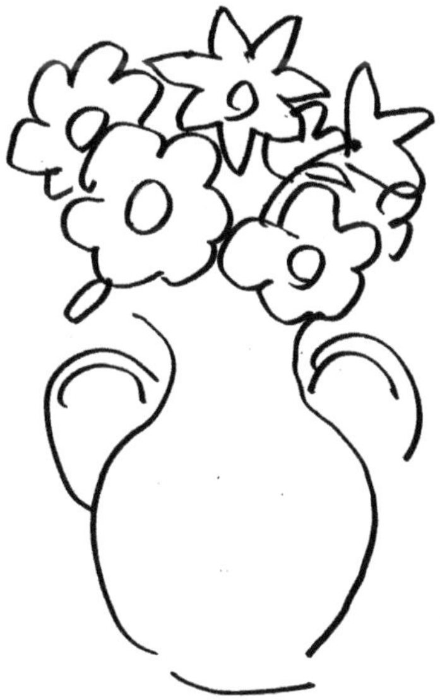

The vase above is based on drawing a letter **S** and its mirror image.

How symmetrical is your rendering? If there is a vase of flowers nearby, stop to look at it. As drawers, we are always compiling a library of remembered images. We store them in our heads, and we can access them with just a pen and paper. We don't have to always work from a living model.

So now let's advance to something more difficult.

Let's draw a person.

Consider these wonderful sketches by a nine-year-old boy with ambitions to design PlayStation characters. They are a rendition of his thought processes.

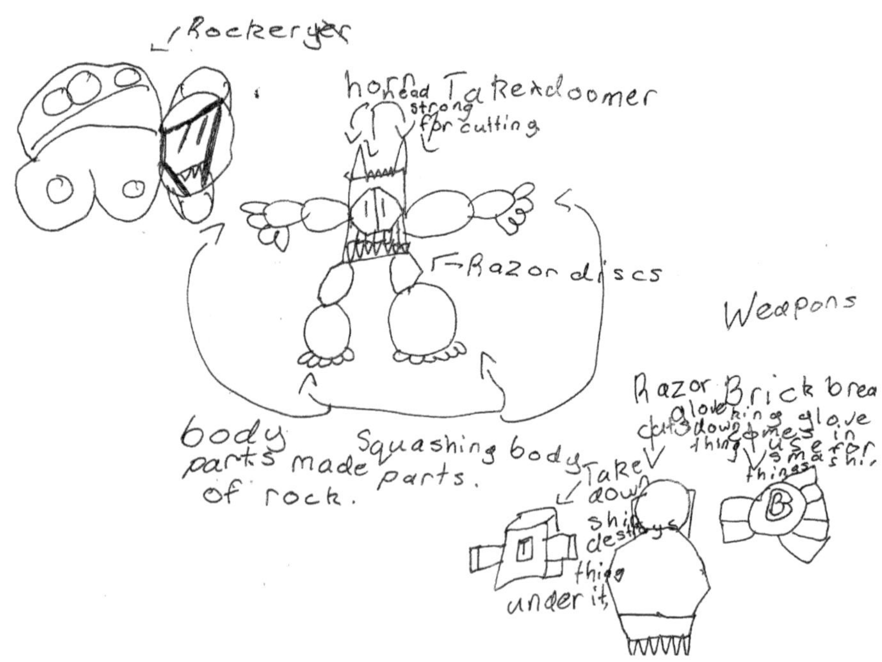

See how in the last example he has even given thought to the weight of the legs. He understands that the figure must be powerful and sturdy on its feet.

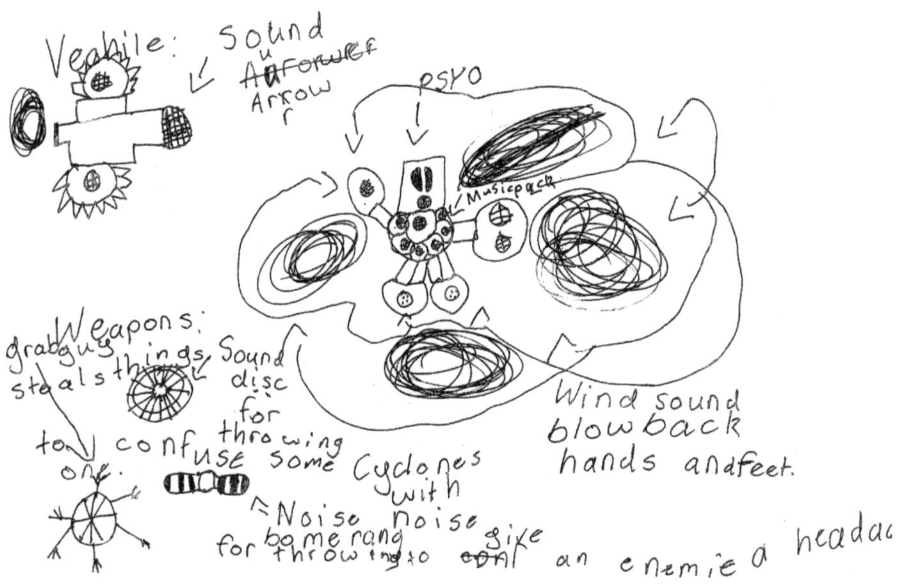

Drawings can be flat and need never leave the page. However, in order to draw something, we have to account for all its component parts. A stick figure is not a representation of a person. Just as an architect begins to plan a structure with a diagram that shows what goes where, we do precisely the same for a drawing of a person. We must account for joints and fingers in our initial ‘map’.

Let us begin with the head.

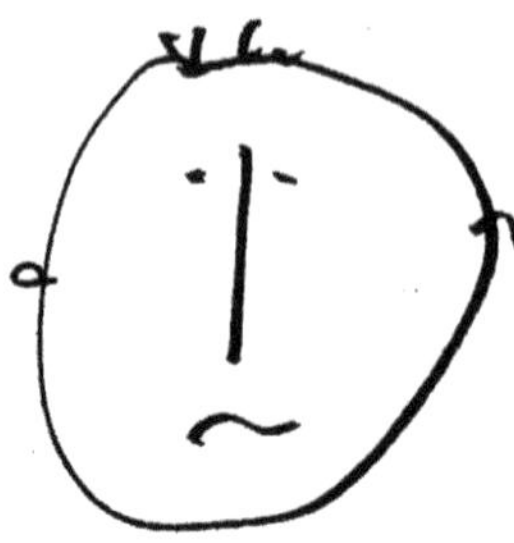

This drawing was done by an adult who claims not to be able to draw. What it shows is a simple lack of observation, which we can see by looking at the ears and eyes.

Now instead of trying to draw a face, write one out using familiar words. Don't simply dash something off like the illustration above. Write in the component parts as if you were filling in a form: *Hair, Forehead, Eye, Eyebrow, Cheek, Nose, Chin, Neck, Ears.*

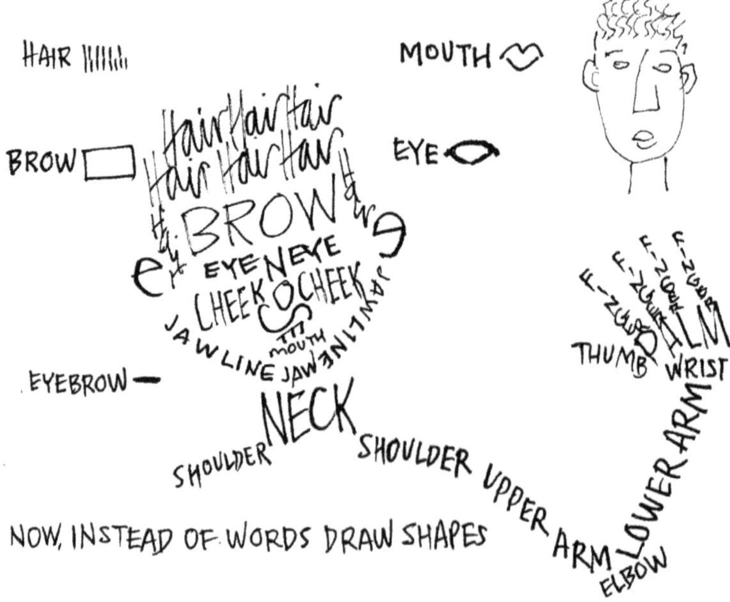

This exercise can be playful – look at the illustration above and see how the word *Nose* has been written.

If you copy the word-face illustration, you will note the playful use of cursive writing to depict hair. Observe how the word *Nose* also breaks out from the writing grid. Four letters have been placed one beneath the other.

When you draw your own version of the word-picture, you essentially become an architect – an architect of everything.

Everything that exists has its own structure, and once we understand the structure, we begin to see far more – everything we can see derives from an alphabet of simple geometrical shapes. They are your building blocks.

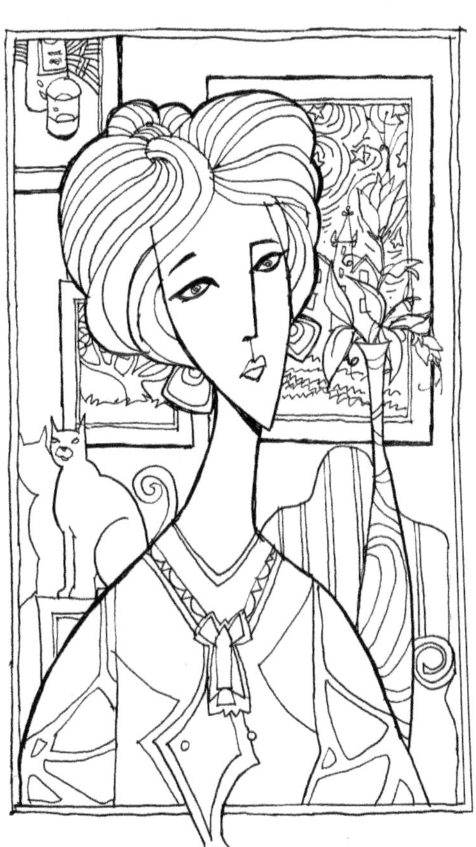

17

HIDDEN PATTERNS

The architecture of everything is based on simple geometry. To draw with confidence, you need to understand how things are constructed.

If you reflect, you will see that universal geometry tells us that everything can be described (or drawn) as constructions of squares, circles and triangles. You don't need complicated formulae or equations.

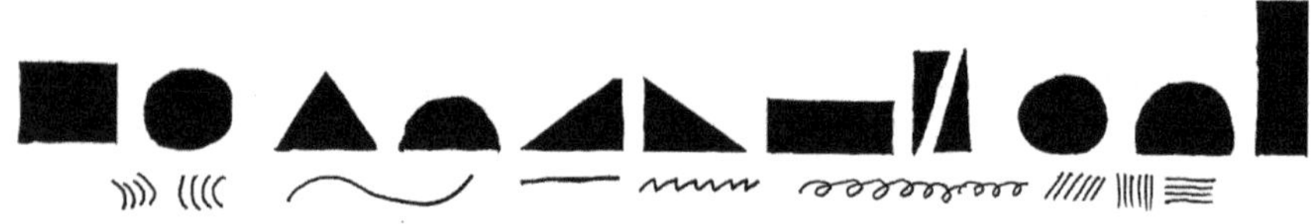

Above are all the shapes you need to construct any living shape, from a person to an animal to a flower. Our world is not random in design. All creatures are constructed from the same essential shapes – nature adheres to basic principles. The dinosaur was ultimately too large, yet it had a skeleton that followed the same basic structure as ours. Even birds follow genetic variations of the same design. As you learn to construct entire people and animals, you will note the similarities between them. A four-legged creature's head is parallel to the earth, similar to ours, which is raised because of our erect posture.

Here are five different animals broken down into simple, easy shapes.

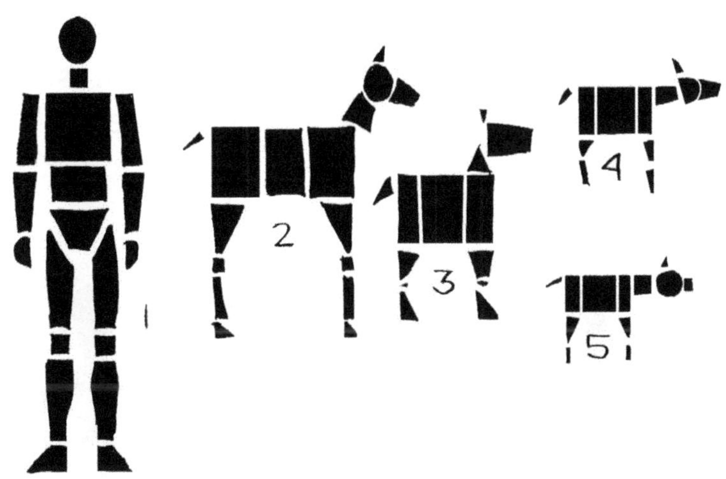

I've shown the human figure front-on and the animals side-on with just two limbs. If I draw the human side-on, on hands and knees, we can see the similar architectural principles at work.

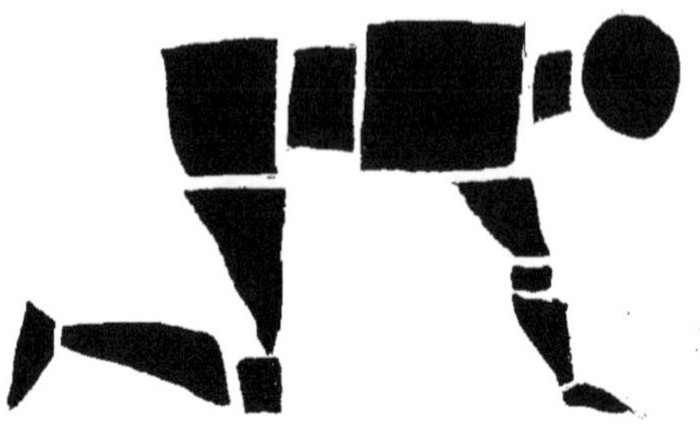

Copy these simple constructions and you are well on your way to drawing convincing pictures.

Once we understand the way these basic shapes are inherent in everything, we can move from drawing people and animals to drawing with greater complexity – flowers, trees, and landscapes. As for animals, four-legged or four-limbed creatures share similar structures: they have a head, two eyes, and so on. Compare the skeleton of a human to that of a dog.

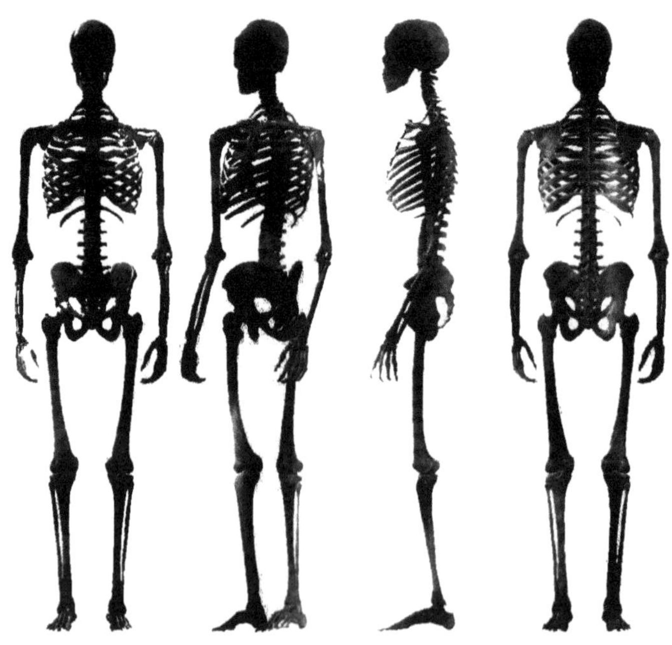

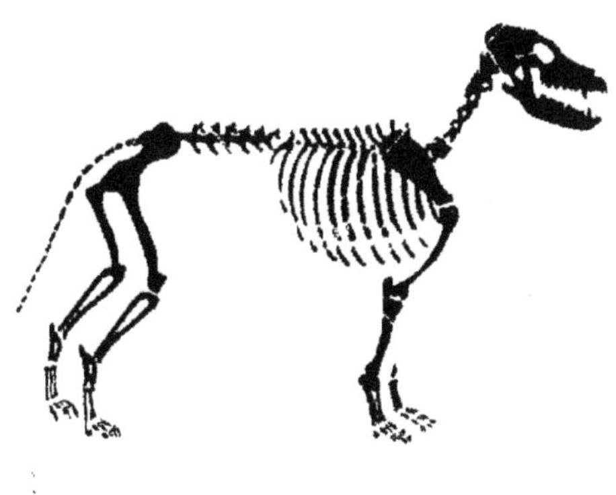

The similarities make the task of drawing them much easier. The skeleton of the dog is similar to any other four-legged animal. What we need is a working understanding of these anatomies. Then, when we examine bird and marine life, we'll see that their architectures are not that far removed from the basic structures we're already familiar with.

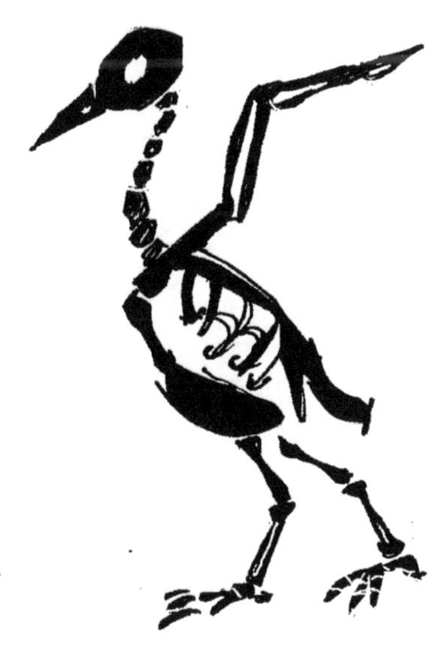

And here is the skeleton of a fish:

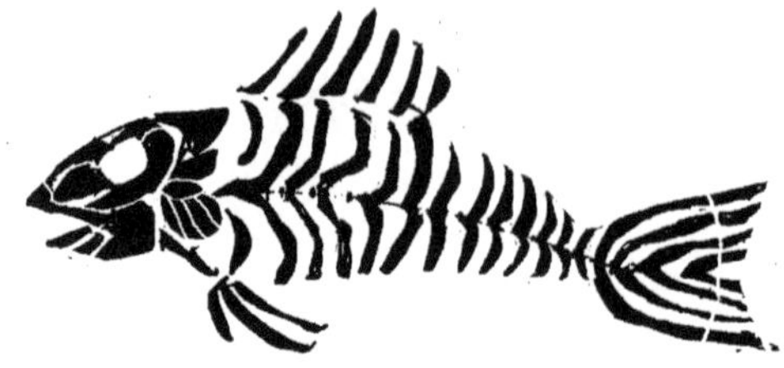

Seeing an object is just a part of observing it.

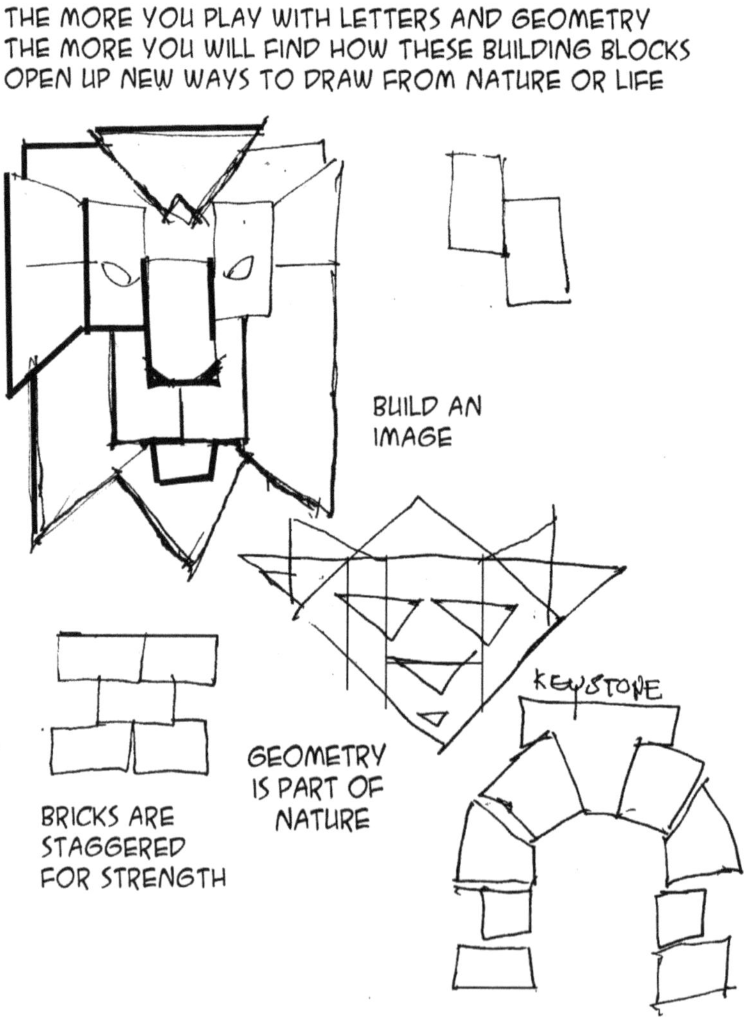

THE MORE YOU PLAY WITH LETTERS AND GEOMETRY
THE MORE YOU WILL FIND HOW THESE BUILDING BLOCKS
OPEN UP NEW WAYS TO DRAW FROM NATURE OR LIFE

BUILD AN
IMAGE

KEYSTONE

GEOMETRY
IS PART OF
NATURE

BRICKS ARE
STAGGERED
FOR STRENGTH

It's beautiful to watch a horse gallop, but once we understand how its body parts unite in that action, the beauty deepens. Each creature is a marvel of creation as well as functionality. When we notice the subtle differences between animals and how they move in their natural environments, we are truly observing like artists.

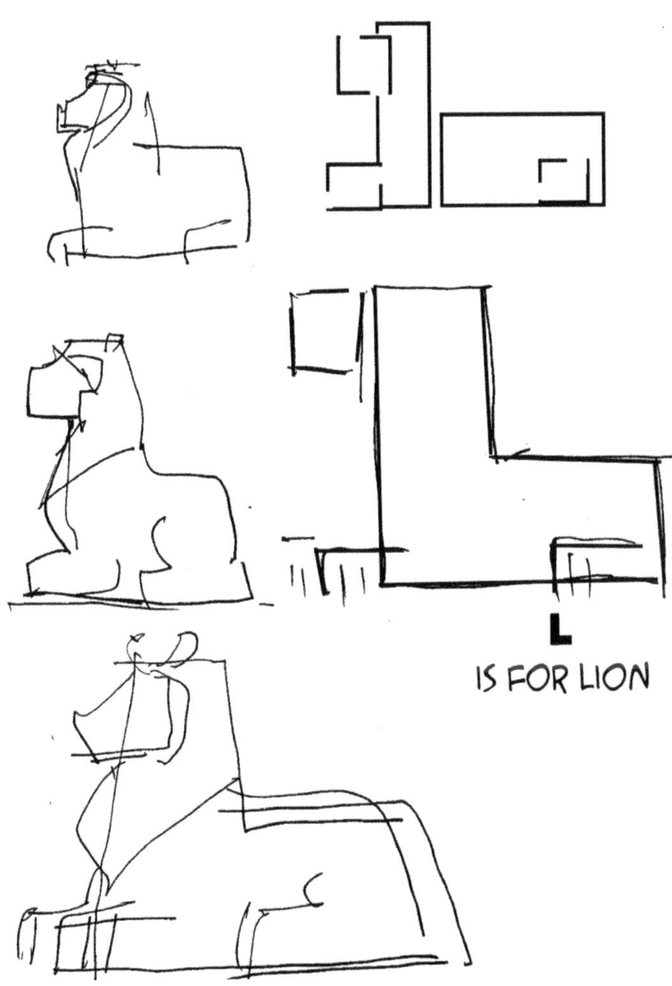

So now that observation has enabled us to establish the architectural rules of the animal world, even aquatic life, we can look at everything else.

18

PATTERNS IN NATURE

In the universe of plants, the rules of geometry apply even more visibly. Anyone can draw a daisy. I bet you've doodled them without even thinking.

They would look something like this:

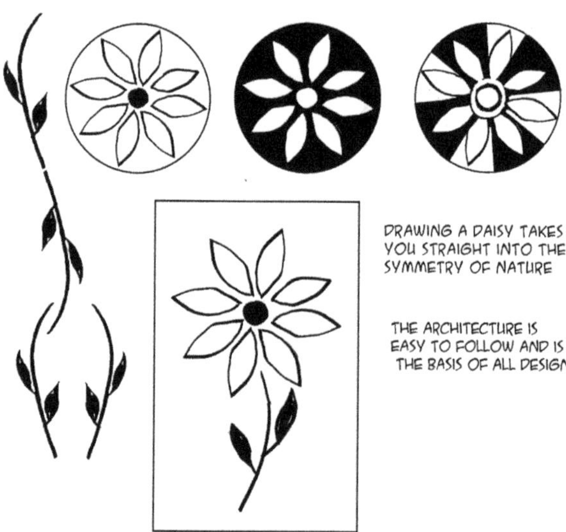

If you follow the rules of how nature operates, your

drawing will immediately look better than your first attempts.

Try to draw a more splendid tree – it will then look something like this:

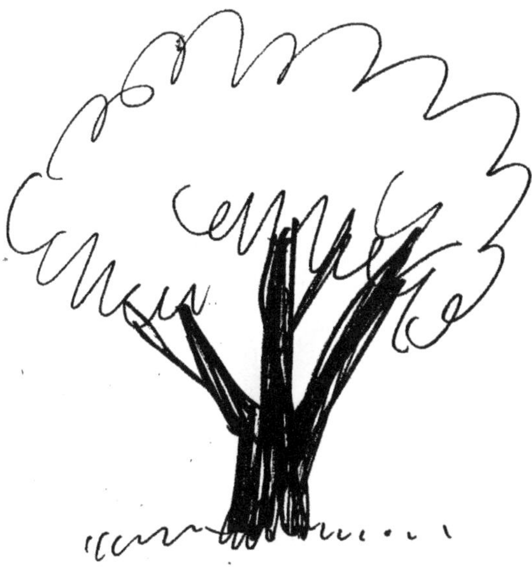

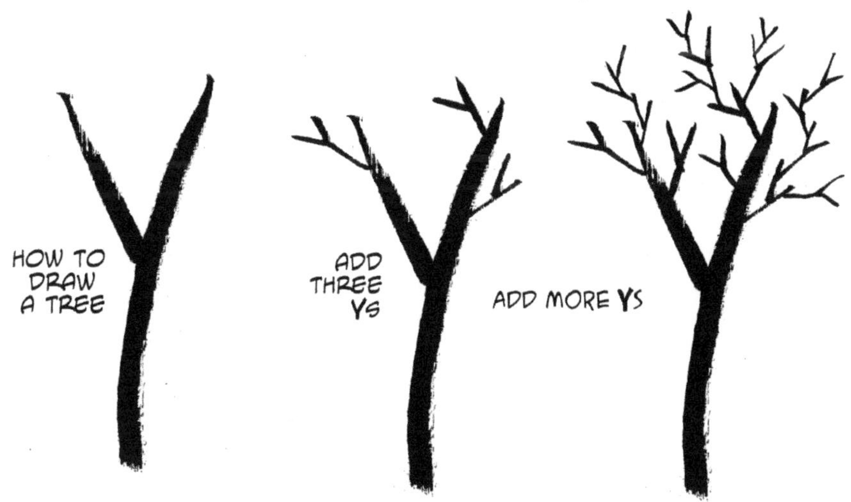

A tree is trickier to draw than a daisy. It begins as a stem and then branches off in many directions. In capturing the elegant symmetry of a tree, what we need is the letter **Y** to assist us. **Y** is a letter that branches off.

Then you can take it further – this time through using the letter **D**.

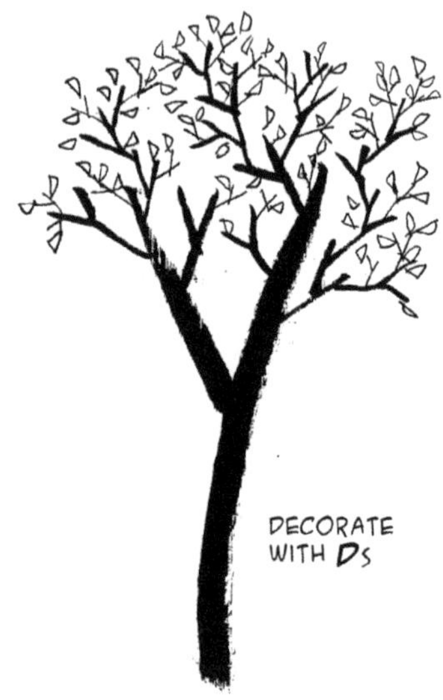

I hope by now you are starting to see that you have all the shapes you need to draw people, animals and a range of natural phenomena.

19

THE DECONSTRUCTED CAT

Once we have learnt a bit about the universal underlying structures of things, we are ready to draw a far more complex illustration – in this case, a cat.

The anatomy of a cat is the same as that of a lion. In fact, learning to draw a cat will help you to draw *any* four-legged creature. Then once we understand the four-limb structure (which includes birds and even fish, when you observe their left-right structure), we begin to appreciate the symmetry and geometry that connects them all.

And if you're wondering why there are so many cats in this book, it's because I've lived with these animals for many years, so I've had the chance to observe them the most.

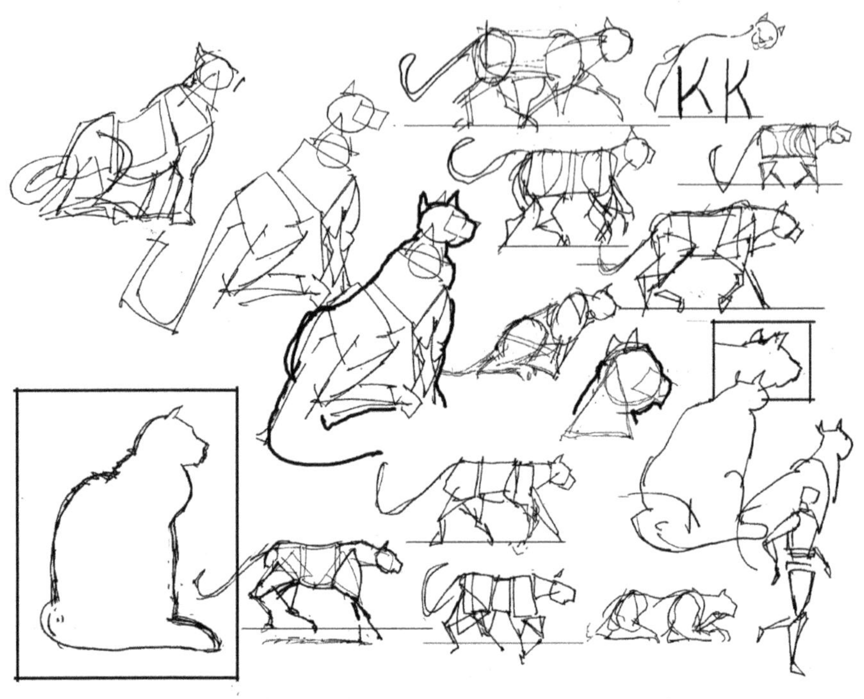

In my illustration of the cat above, I wanted to show you the process I went through to construct it. I wanted you to mentally take it apart – in an act of deconstruction.

Can you see how the deconstruction reveals that everything is based on geometry?

The process of constructing a cat on a page is also a guide to how an illustration of a cat can be *deconstructed* – which entails a stripping away of details to expose the underlying geometry of the cat.

Look at the silhouette of the cat in the lower left corner. For a start, you can't see any paws. The cat is sitting on her haunches, yet they too are hidden. Because this is all in silhouette, we cannot tell whether the cat is facing us or not. In your mind's eye, you will actually see a complete 'picture' of the cat.

If you attempted to draw the silhouette without first examining the sketches – or plans – that lead to a full view of the cat, your silhouette would probably lack accuracy. You need to understand the *architecture* of the animal to be able to draw it as one looped line.

To draw well, we must think first. A good drawing requires thought. But in order to understand drawing, you must actually draw. So copy all the drawings you encounter here. Draw them more than once.

Copying is how we learn to draw. Thinking is the bonus.

20

LESSONS FROM A MASTER

When you started this book, you thought you couldn't draw. Now you should have the confidence to draw people, animals and plants. You're ready to get even bolder. You can begin to draw anything.

Let's say you wanted to draw a man standing in a field looking up at the sky. Something like this:

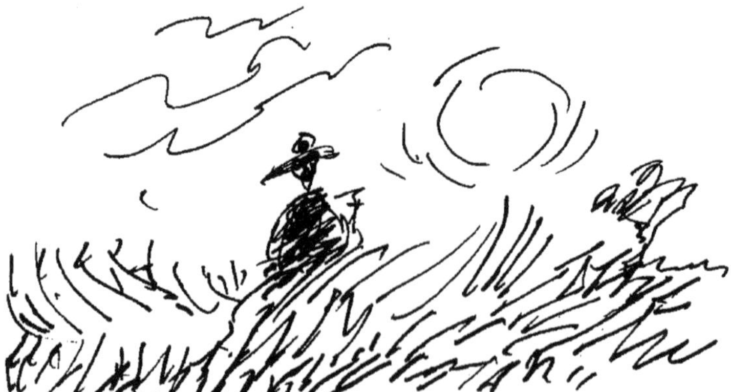

This sketch is based on Vincent van Gogh's unique paintings. I've copied the *style* of his drawing. Note how simply he seems to do it. Copy these copies. Better still, find the originals, or prints, and copy those.

Now we are in a position to deconstruct the manner in which Van Gogh drew by looking at the simple strokes and shapes he used. Van Gogh's paintings are assemblies of simple lines and shapes. What follows are copies of his drawings – drawn in his style.

Study and copy.

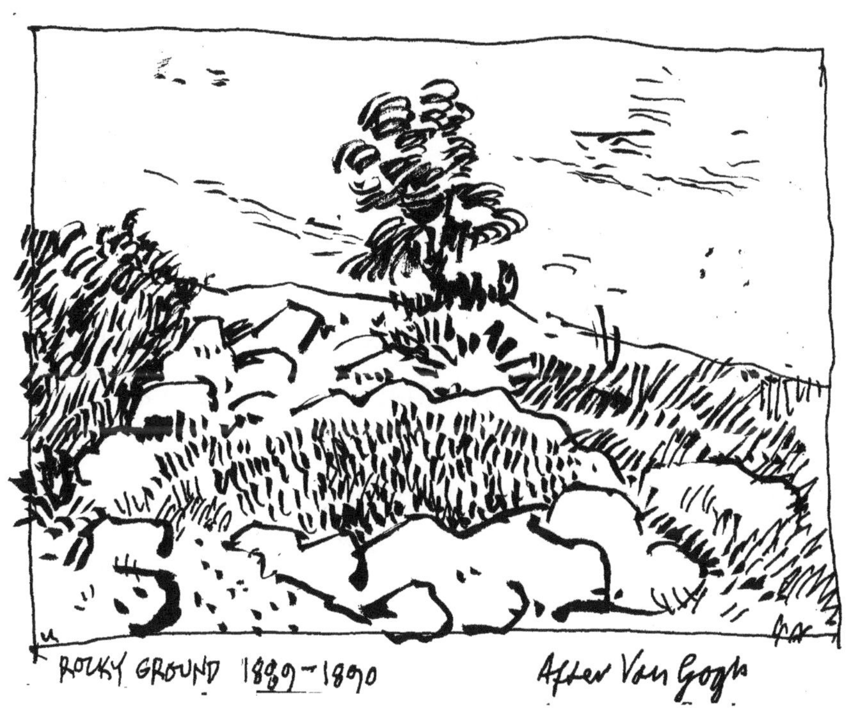

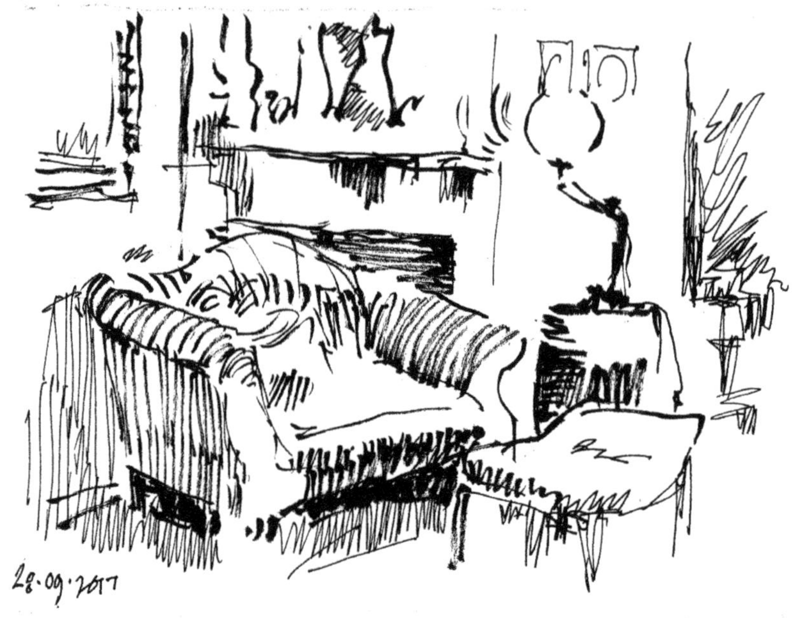

Think of any drawing as an assemblage of small units.

Pablo Picasso and Henri Matisse were also artists who could reduce an image to just one line.

But of all the great masters of drawing, none is more accessible than Van Gogh. This is a further *copy* of another of Vincent's originals:

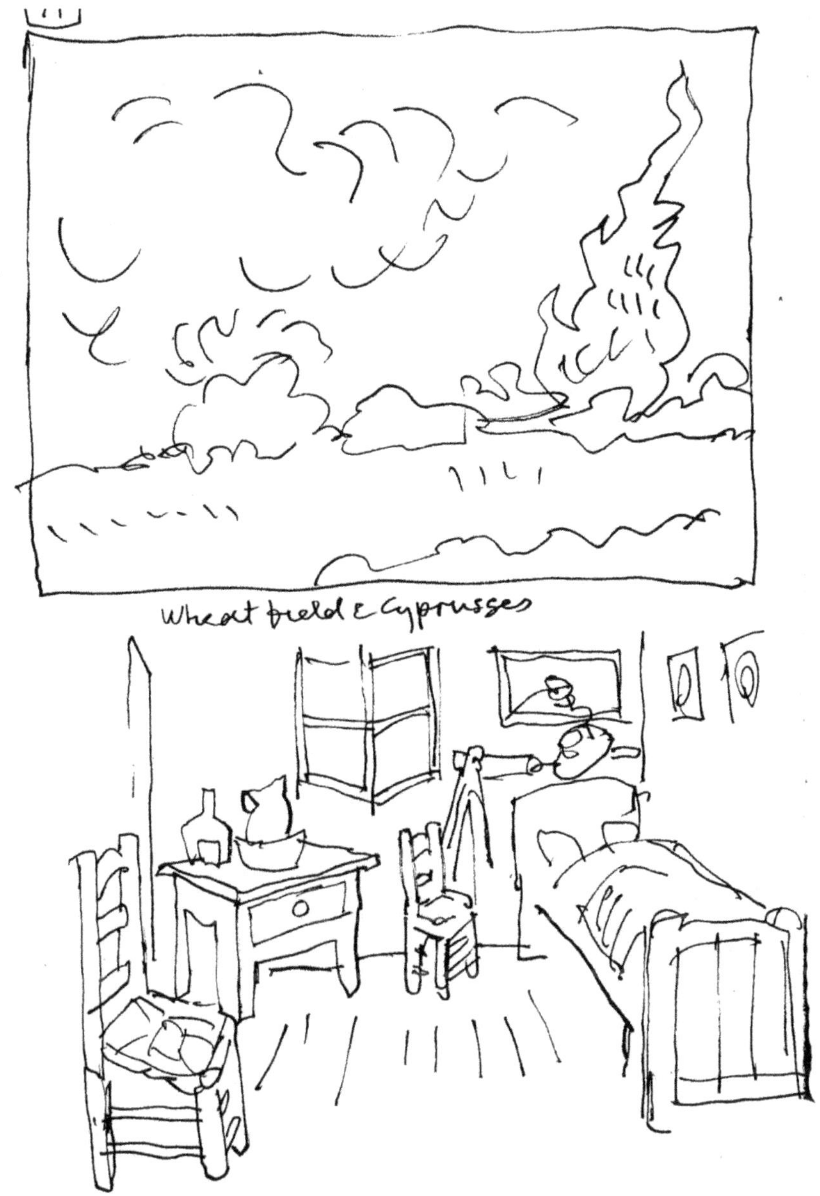

For now, work in small patches. Isolate and identify shapes. Notice how often the shape (and letter) **S** comes up.

Now it's your turn to copy.

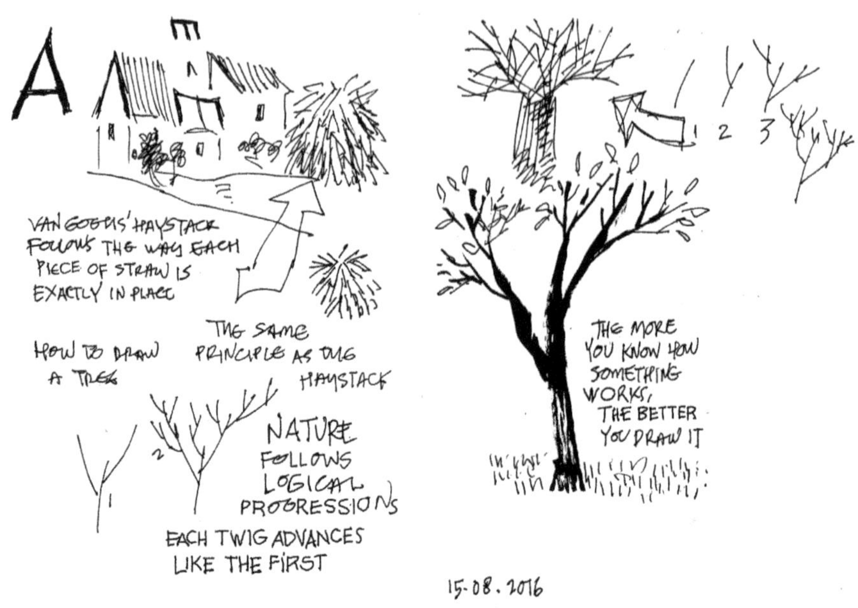

Here are some easy landscapes and still-life pictures to copy and boost your confidence.

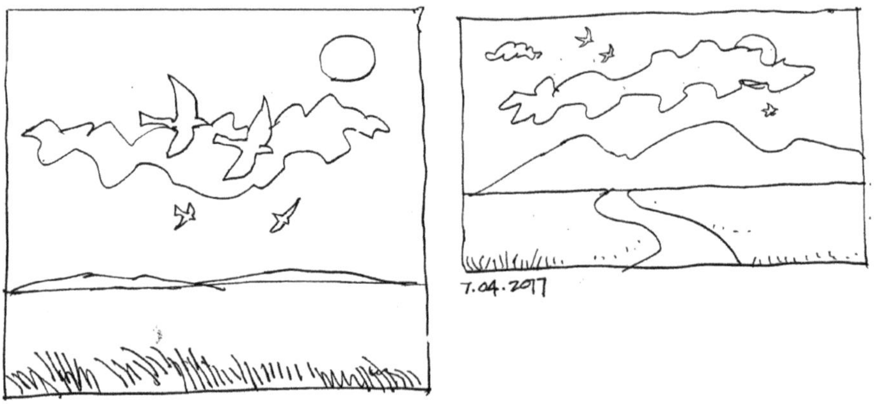

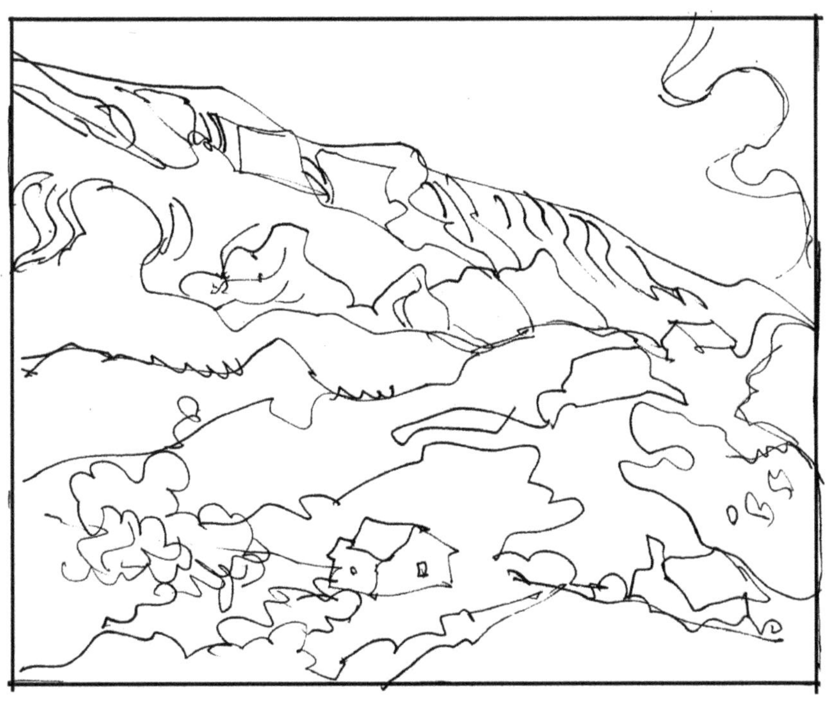

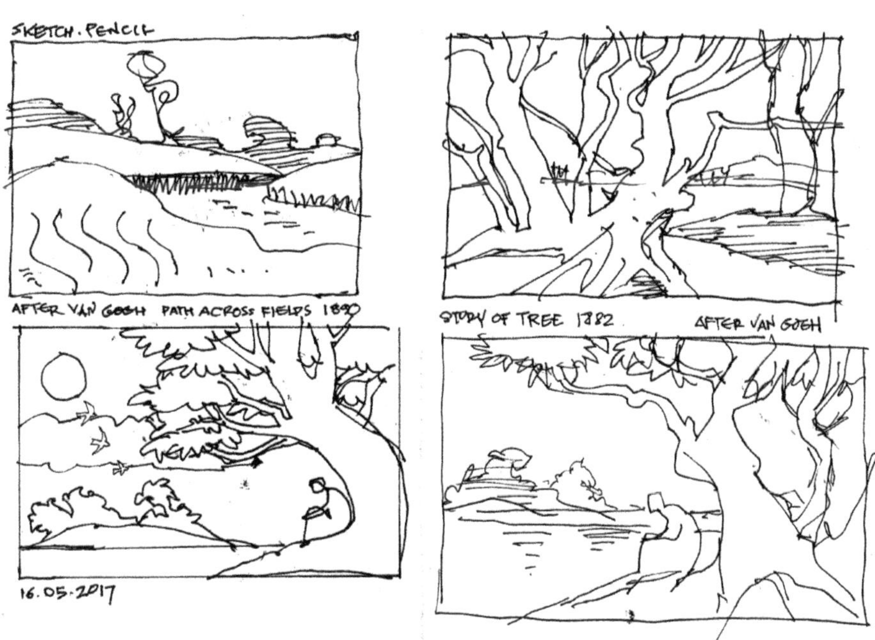
SKETCH. PENCIL
AFTER VAN GOGH PATH ACROSS FIELDS 1890
STUDY OF TREE 1882
AFTER VAN GOGH
16.05.2017

The two bottom sketches are inspired by the tree above them.

It's now time to combine our elements and put figures into landscapes.

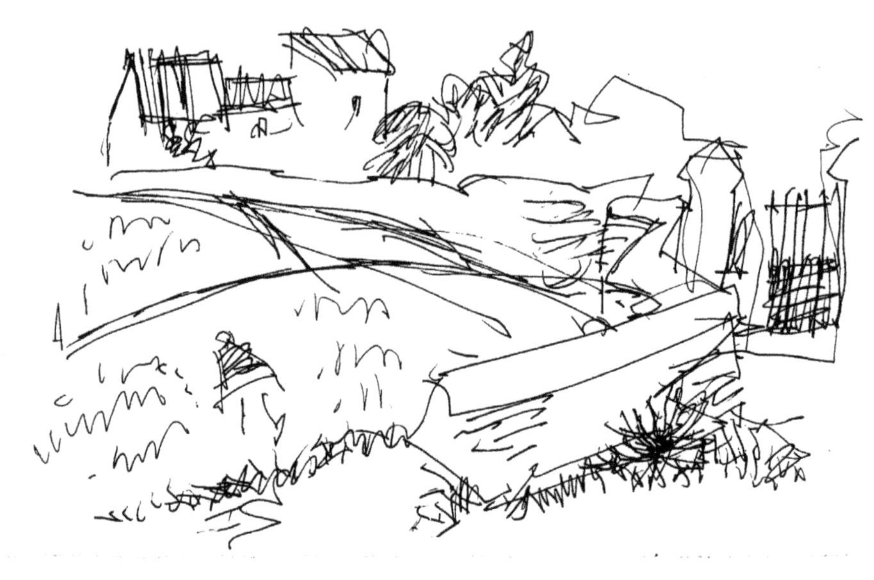

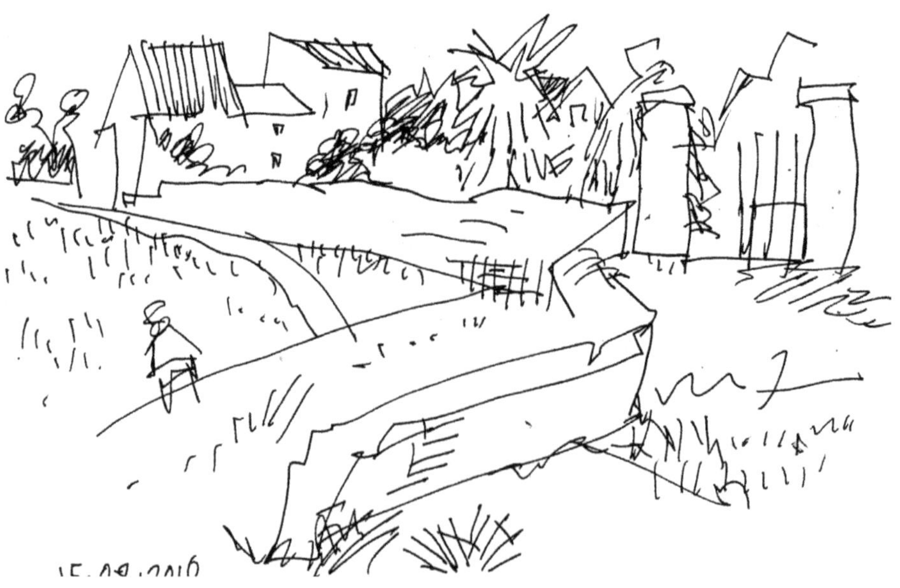

21

TEXTURE

Once we've understood the object we are drawing and we can draw it – at least in basic form – we want to add details to it to bring it alive. This is what we call texture.

Texture is a series of repetition that makes our drawings more vivid.

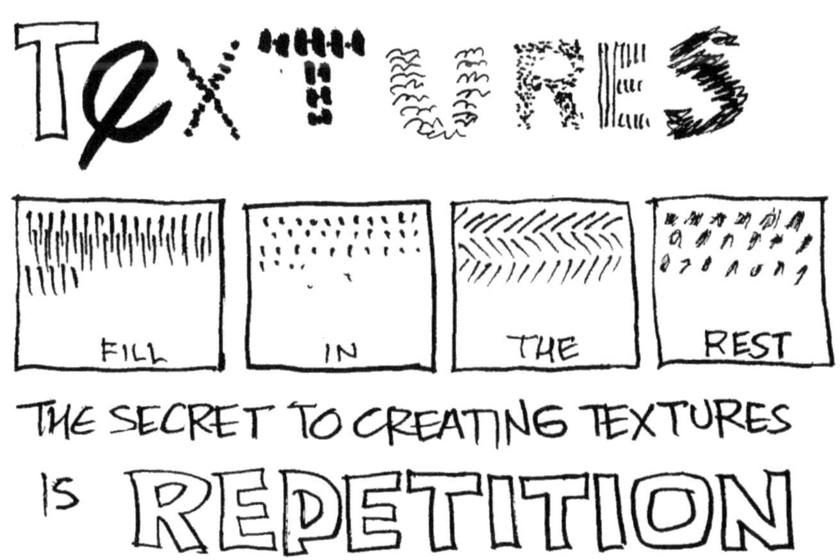

Study and copy the above examples. All they are are a variety of simple pen or brushstrokes, repeated.

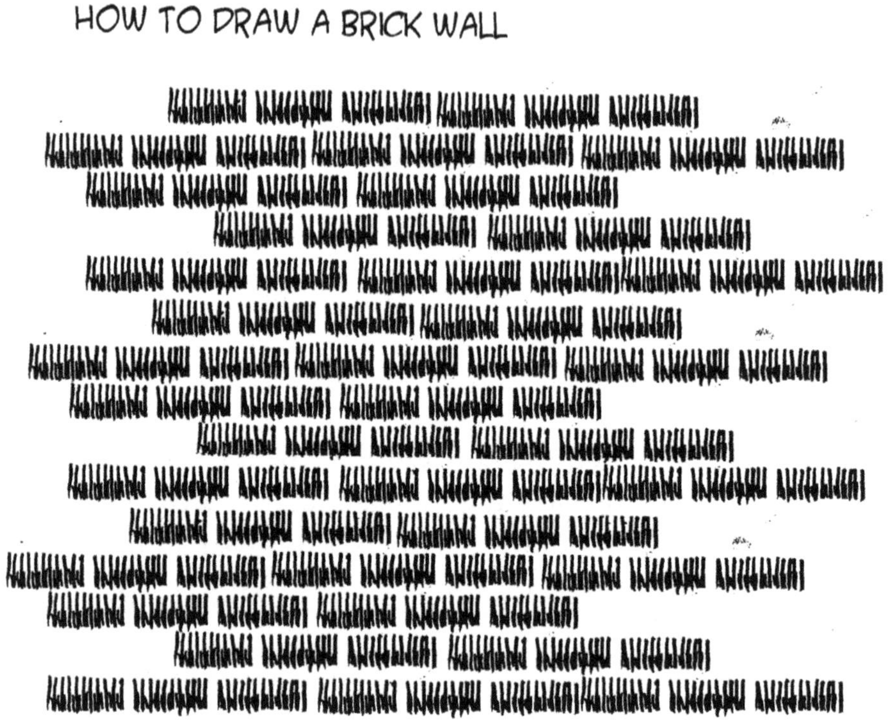

HOW TO DRAW A BRICK WALL

By adding different textures, we are able to give our drawing a completely different feel. Notice the difference in each of these.

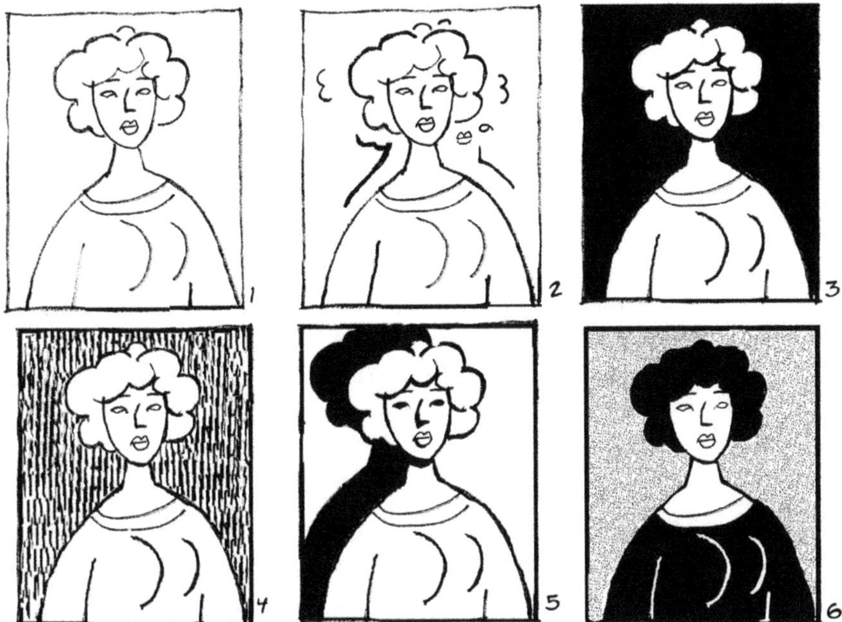

I now want to talk about the instrument with which you draw. You've probably been using pens such as ballpoints or fineliners. But to improve the spectrum of your abilities, we need to talk about the brush as a drawing option.

In the days before animal rights the best brushes for fine work favoured particularly by cartoonists and comic book illustrators were Kolinsky sable hair brushes. The brush comes from the tail of the sable – it's always been my hope that the animals were sheared, rather than slaughtered. Drawing with a brush is a more subtle exercise than drawing with a fineliner. A good brush retains moisture and can taper to a point. It also allows the drawing of a line thinner than a hair and with applying just the gentlest pressure, spread in width. It allows spearhead-shaped leaves to be drawn in just one brushstroke.

This takes us straight into the heart of Chinese and Japanese writing and drawing. In both Eastern cultures, there is little distinction between writing and drawing. Both are practised with a brush. A page of calligraphy is revered as much as a drawing. They are inseparable and the rules of writing a letter are precisely those employed in drawing. The same ritual approach is applied to both exercises.

The Chinese American writer, philosopher and painter Mai-Mai Sze produced a scholarly work called *The Tao of Painting*. Taoism centres on the oneness of everything. Yin and yang, though opposites, form an entirety joined in one whole.

Using this as a framework, let's move now into drawing. There is both symmetry and geometry that connects the brushstroke of the leaf to a principle in nature. The geometry of the alphabet is to be found in nature. Paul Cézanne, the painter, defined it thus: 'Treat nature in terms of the cylinder, the sphere, and the cone, the whole put into perspective'.

If I asked you to draw a large rectangular building and an oak tree, and I gave you a pen and brush, which would you use to draw which? There is, of course, a natural link between brush and tree as there is a logic to designing buildings with draughting pens. I spent two miserable years studying to be an architect where a pen then called a Rapidograph was the acknowledged preferred tool of the trade. That pen contributed somewhat to my misery. One can draw wonderful trees with the spawn of the Rapidograph. All drawing instruments in the hand of a master are malleable. But my own preferred, natural way of drawing (my Tao) is a more forgiving, pliant partner. Your drawing instrument of preference is a marriage.

Mai-Mai Sze has left an amazing record of Chinese drawing. She has given us a dictionary of Chinese drawing techniques. These are my copies of her lessons.

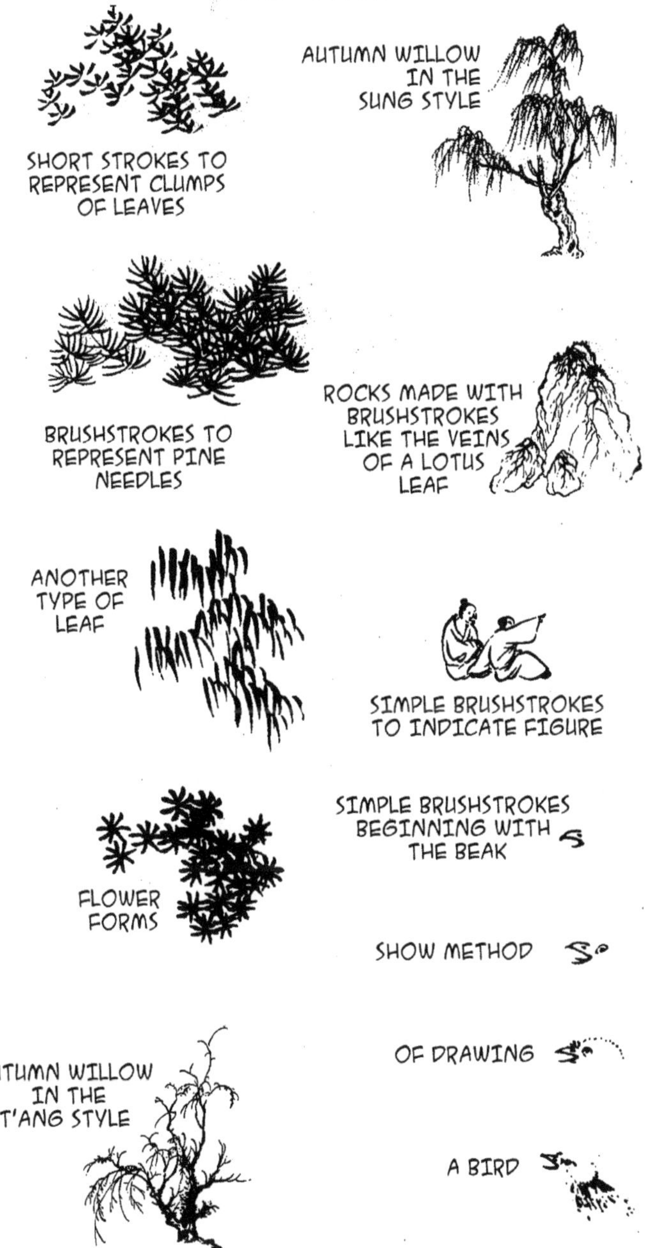

Van Gogh was a great student of Japanese and Chinese brush art.

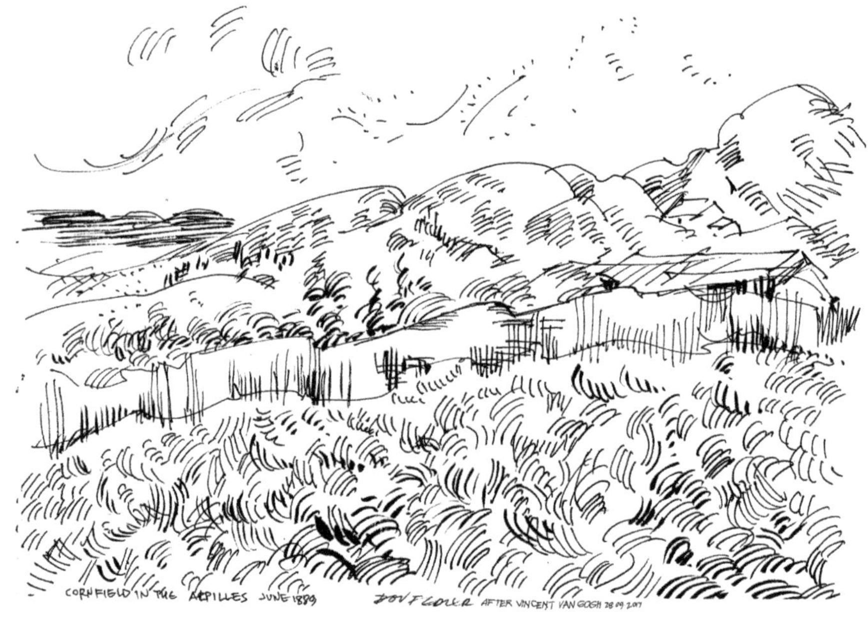

The picture above is drawn from life but follows the methodology of Mai-Mai Sze as well as Van Gogh's method.

It really is as easy as it looks.

If you copy these textures, they will add to your visual vocabulary.

Before we advance to adding more than lines to our drawings, try and draw something of your own invention – applying all the lessons you have learnt so far.

Copy a photograph or draw from your imagination. Try and break down the figures or objects in your drawing into simple letters, lines or shapes. I prefer to copy from great masters (such as Paul Cézanne and Amedeo Modigliani) but a photo of your own is as good a place to begin. Copy them first to give you inspiration and momentum. Bear in mind that by 'copy', I mean exactly that – the rendition of an idea, not a line-for-line imitation.

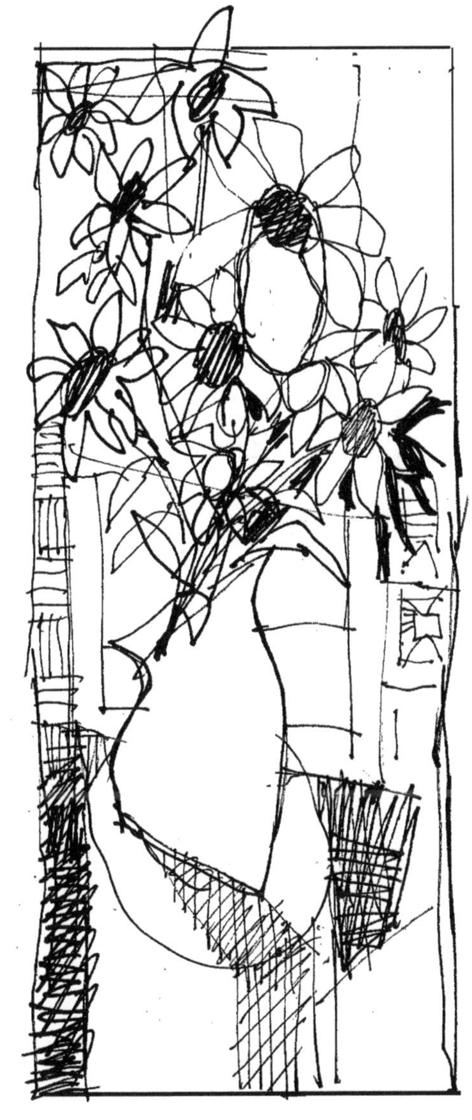

The vase of flowers is from my own sketchbook. Look for inspiration in your own work.

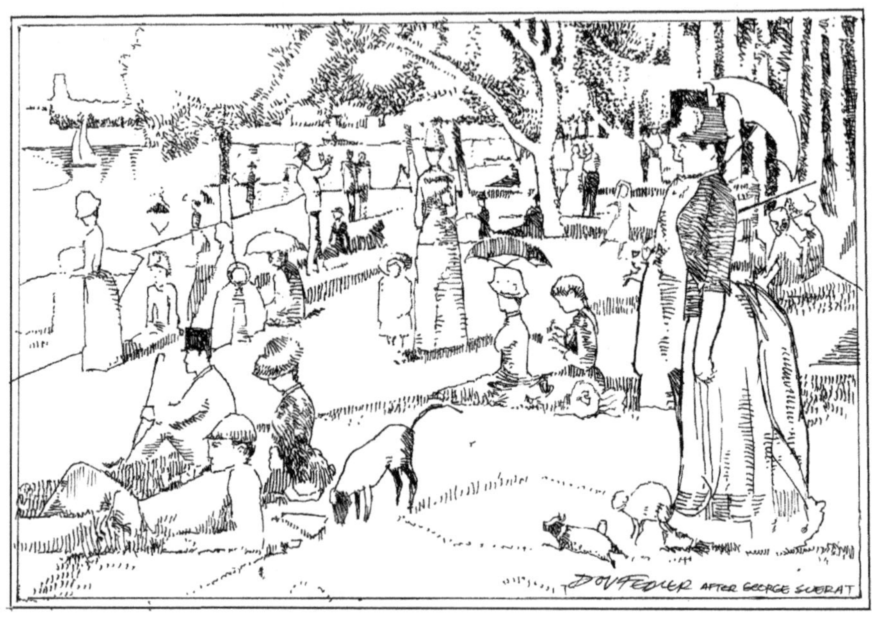

This is a copy of a famous painting by the pointillist painter Georges Seurat, who painted in pixels. His drawings follow precise geometry. He is a perfect artist to study beyond just this one painting. Search for examples of his art. Note the careful construction of his figures and his intricate use of textures.

In chapter 24, I will show you how to copy this painting using letters from the alphabet.

Have a look at how I have used texture in the cartoon below to denote the ripples on the water, the beard, the stones, the rockiness of the island.

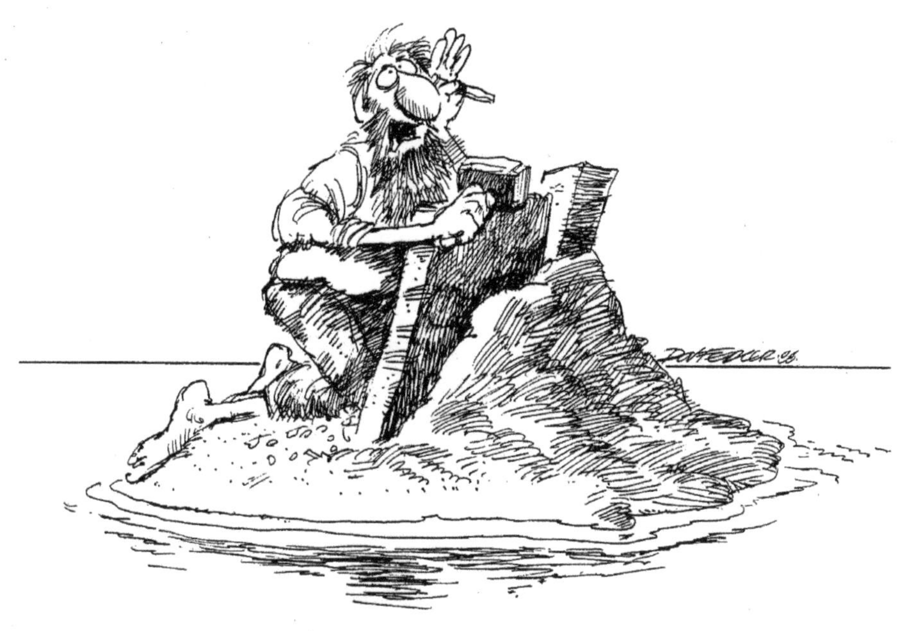

'COME AGAIN – THOU SHALT NOT WHAT?'

If you have grasped the principles I've shared here about how to break things down into easily recognizable shapes or letters, and if you understand the basic architecture of people and objects, you will always find fresh ways to draw everything.

22

THE HARMONY OF OPPOSITES

Have a look at these three images:

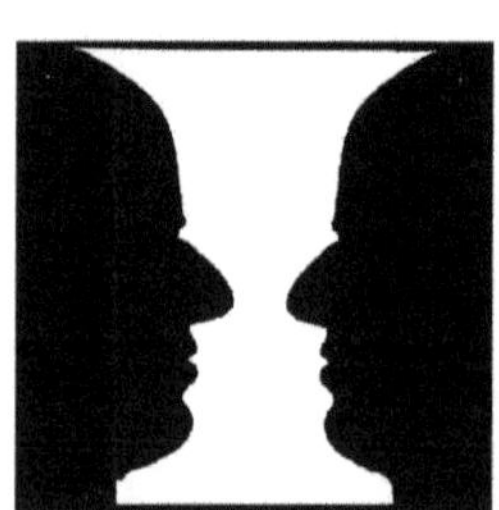

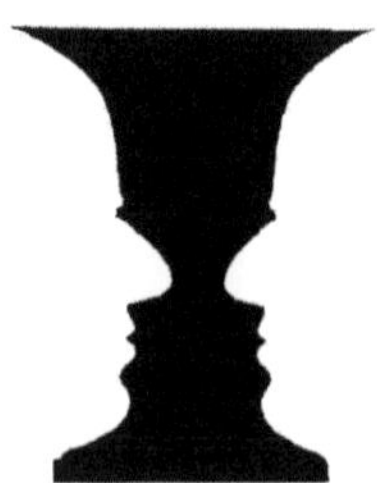

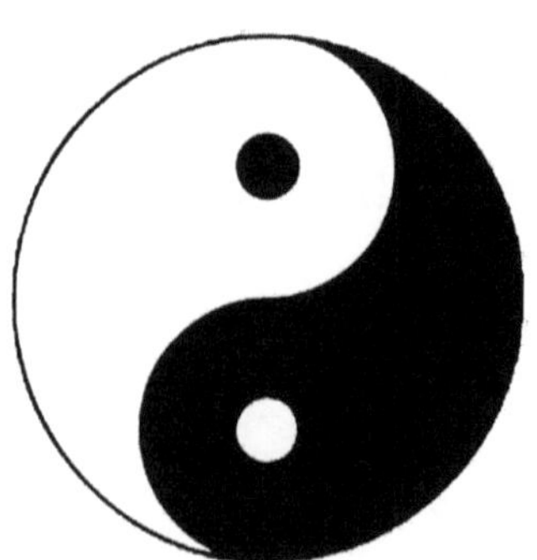

Do you see how the black and white parts play off each other?

In the first example, there appear to be two heads facing each other. Switching white for black and vice versa, a third image appears – a goblet. The sharp contrast of black against white introduces an ambiguity.

I'm sure most of you are familiar with the yin-yang symbol. Yin and yang are opposites that balance each other. The word yin means shady side and yang, sunny side. Yin yang is the concept of duality forming a whole. The symbol for yin yang is called the Taijitu.

How does the deep philosophy underpinning these ideas apply to drawing? Well, think about it like this: every time we place a black mark on a white (or light) page, we are making a yin/yang statement. If you acknowledge that not only have you made marks on a page but that the spaces around these marks also have a purpose or a function, you begin to see more possibilities in front of you. You can fill in these spaces, or leave them as they are. As soon as we fill in the spaces, our drawings begin to inhabit positive and negative space.

Filled in, or filled around, the images take on a more substantial form. They demand to be taken seriously. This phenomenon is easily illustrated with this word example. The options where the lettering or background are in black are the more commanding. This is a primary lesson in light and shadow.

TAKE ME
SERIOUSLY

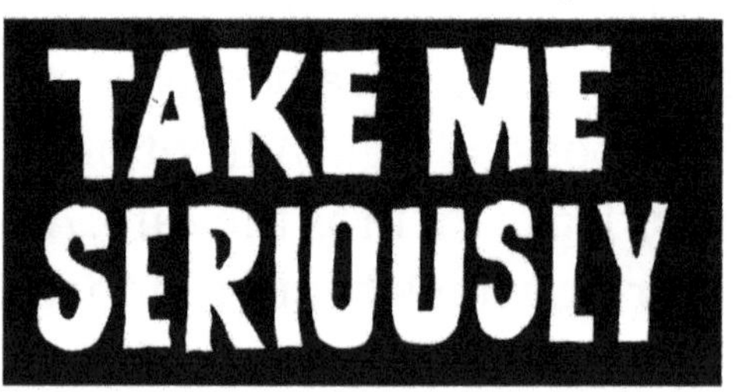

TAKE ME
SERIOUSLY

Now follow the progression of the next sketch.

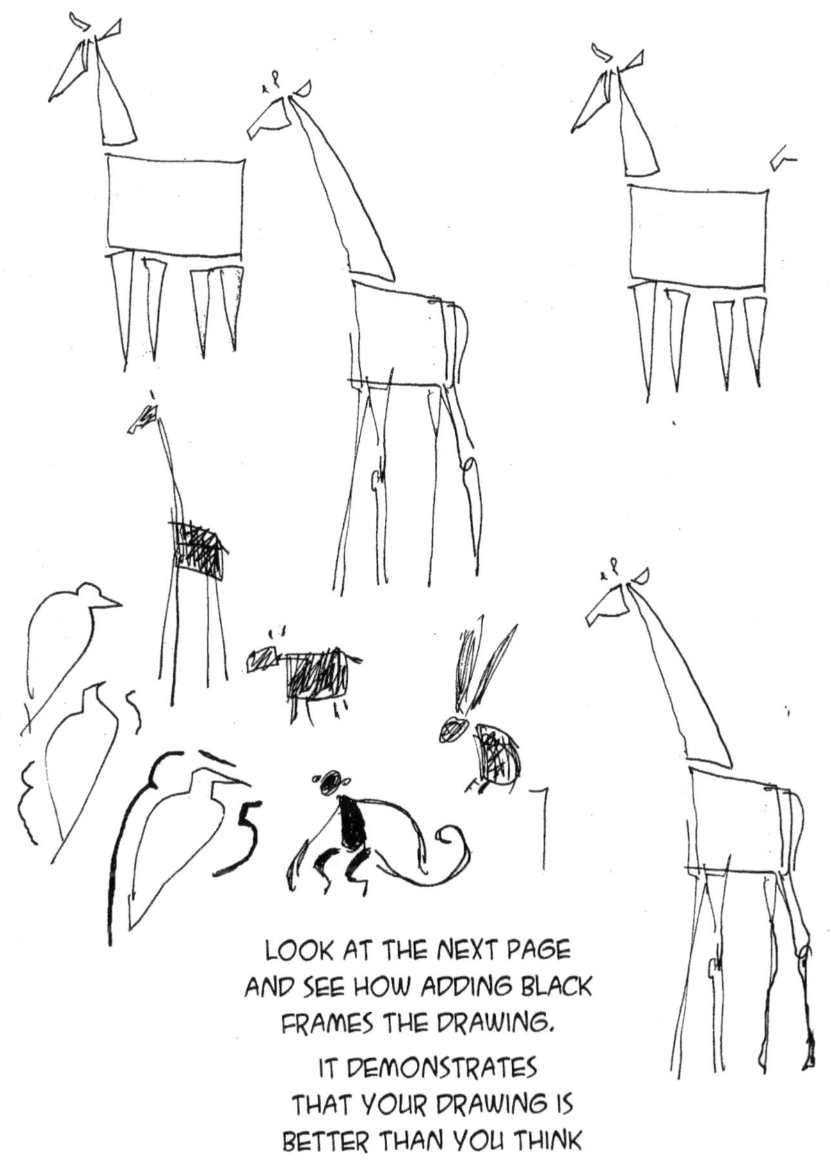

Black adds drama – it introduces light and shadow. Let's play with that concept a little further.

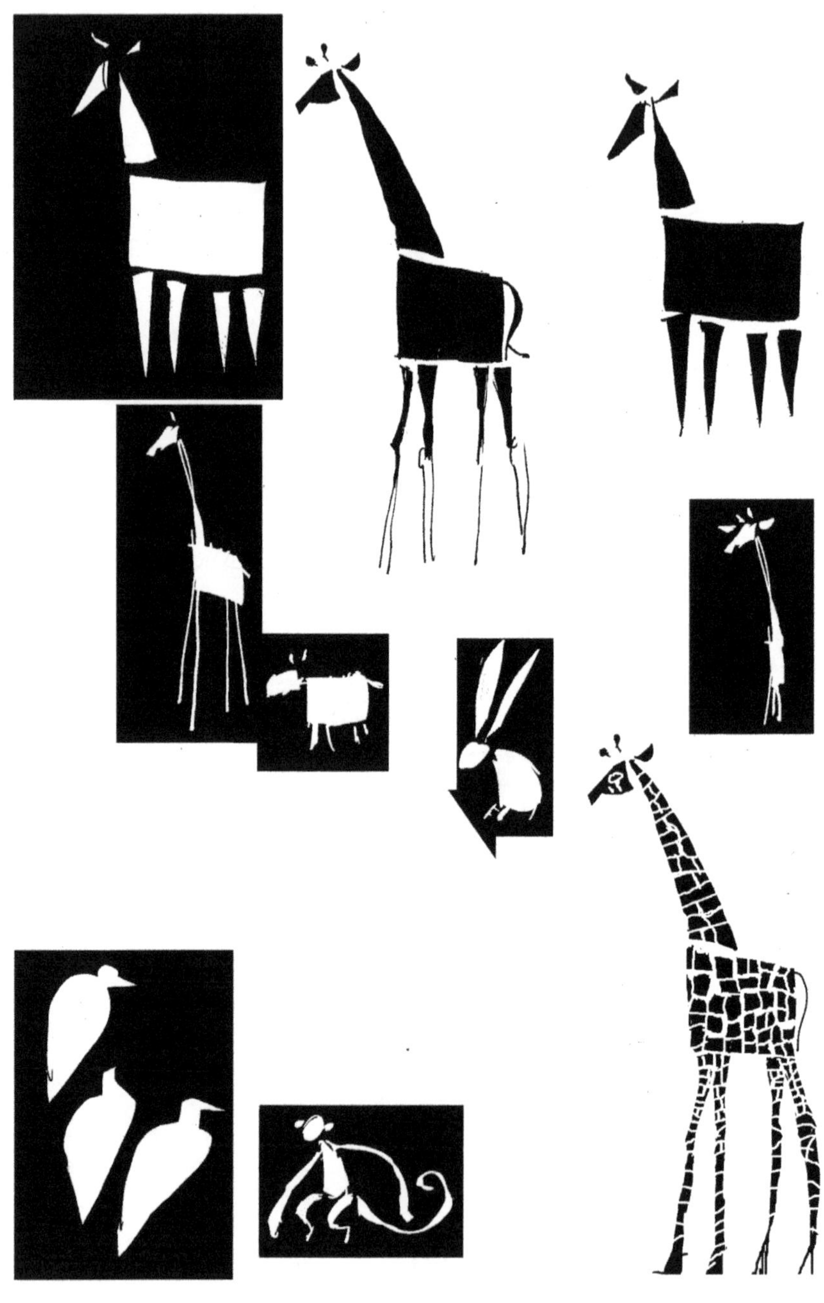

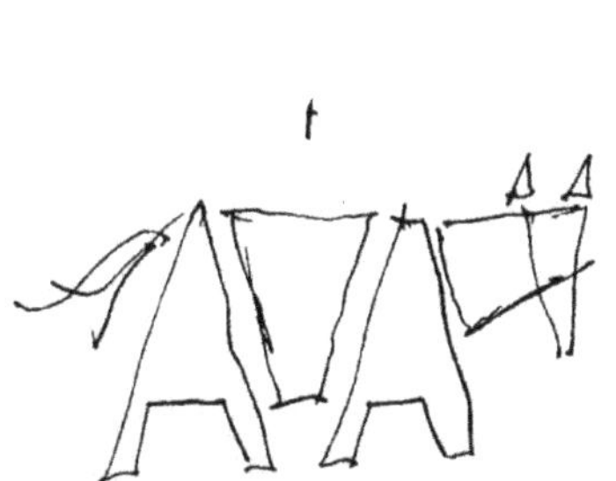

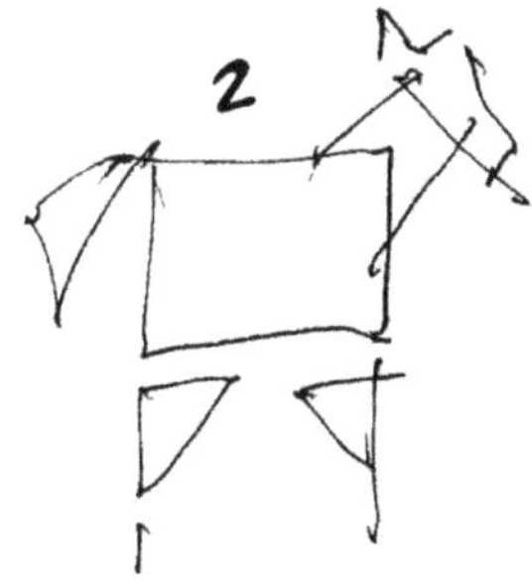

IF YOU UNDERSTAND BASIC ANIMAL STRUCTURE, YOU CAN CONSTRUCT ONE WITH JUST ONE LETTER.

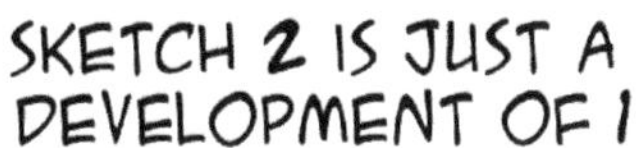

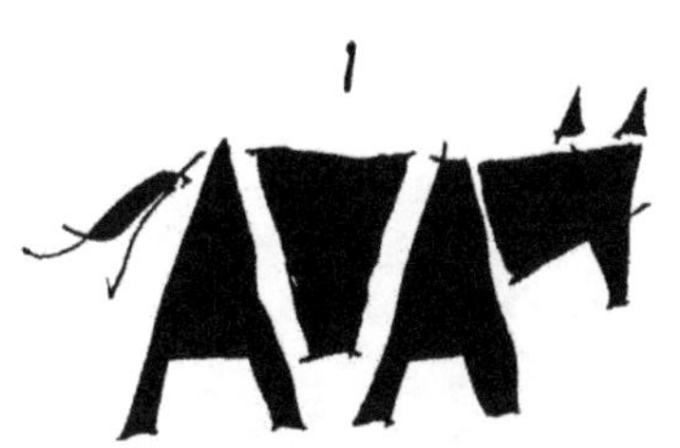

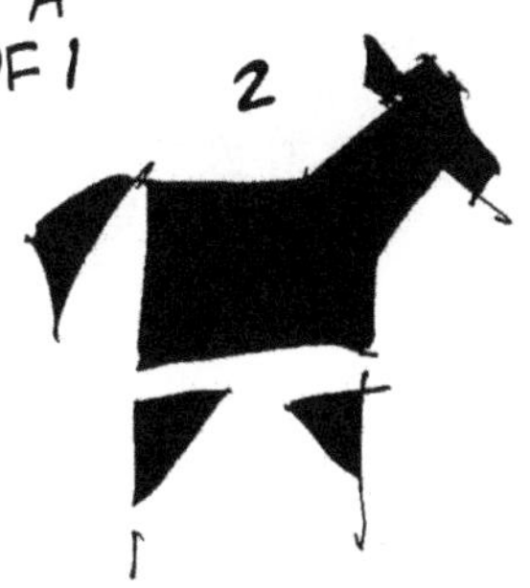

FILLING THE DRAWINGS IN BLACK TAKE US FURTHER INTO THE WORLD OF DESIGN

Your first drawing is a plan for another. The idea is to play with what you have first drawn – then to take it further. See if you can use the ideas of light and shadow to experiment with what is gathering on the page in front of you.

WHAT CAUGHT THIS ARTIST'S EYE
WAS THE HINT OF THE LINE PROTRUDING
FROM THE ANIMAL'S SNOUT

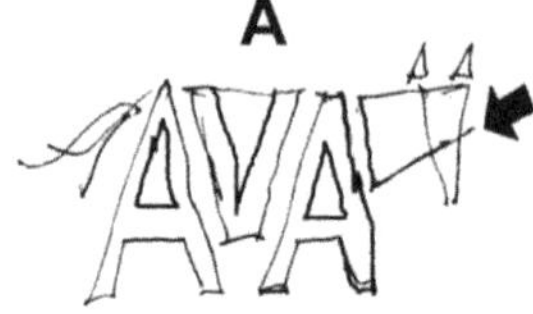

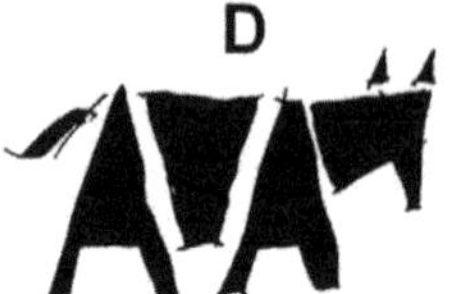

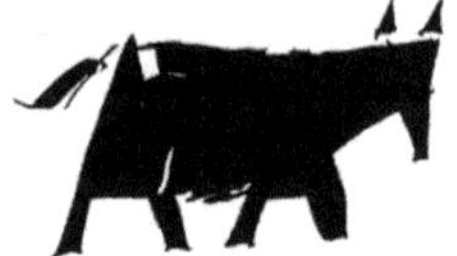

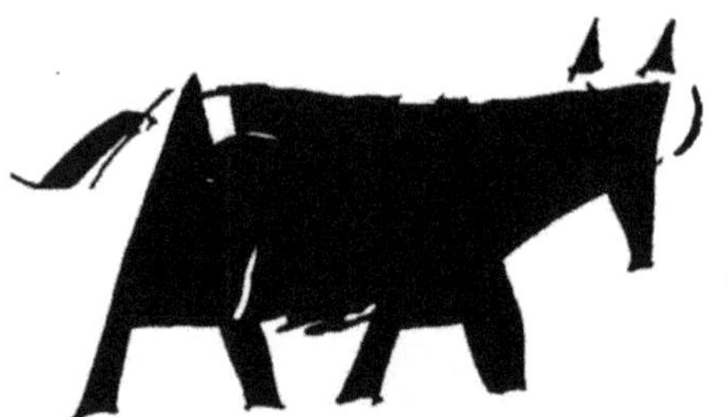

IT SUGGESTED A
WARTHOG.

MORE OBSERVATION
BECAME NECESSARY

AGAIN, PROPORTIONS
HAVE TO FEEL RIGHT

BETTER BUT A
LONG WAY TO
GO YET

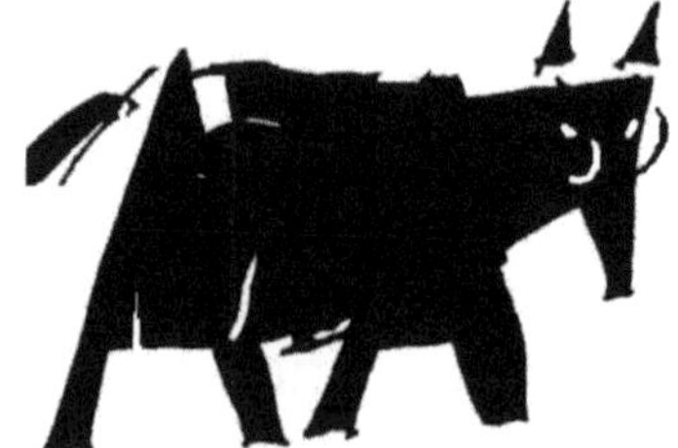

WHATEVER THIS IS
FOR NOW, IT'S
BEEN FUN

23

COME OVER TO THE FAR SIDE

Now we are ready to play with another technique, one that will take our one-dimensional drawings into a new space and help us build complexity.

To begin, place a dark shape behind a light one. This gives us light, shadow and depth.

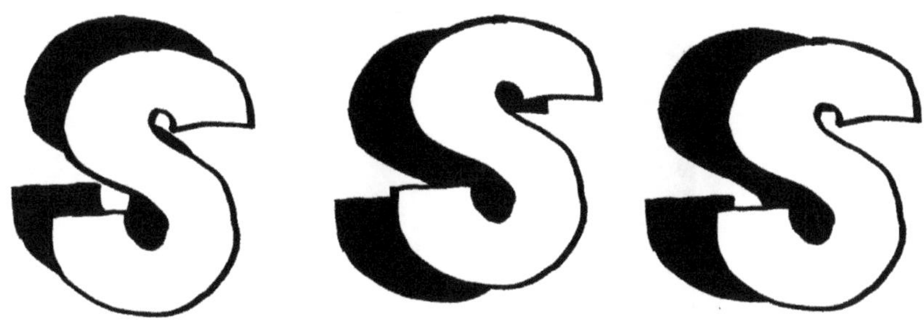

Look at how different the three letter **S** become. Each occupies a particular position in space. This overlapping takes us into the third dimension – and we are about to enter that dimension.

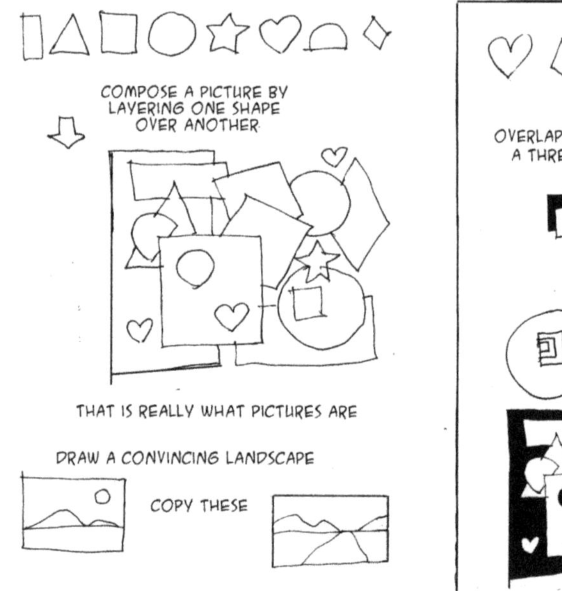

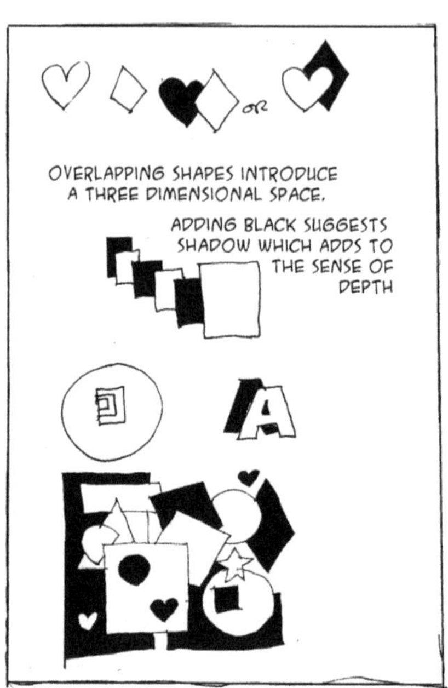

Examine the rectangles below.

Your eye tells you that the white rectangle sits in front of the black one. When we start thinking in terms of 'front' and 'back', we are in the dimension of space. And that is where perspective exists.

I want you to remember that a drawing of space is an illusion – a drawing exists on a surface – it is two dimensional. It does not exist in space. That is the illusion we are about to examine closely.

I have found that people are intimidated by the notion of perspective in drawing because it requires some geometry. Let me see if I can simplify it for you and remove that stigma.

Think simply of the letter **Y**. It is your best friend when it comes to understanding perspective. It offers us a bird's view of an object or place – changing our mental perspective of looking at an object flat-on to one of looking down from above to a space beyond.

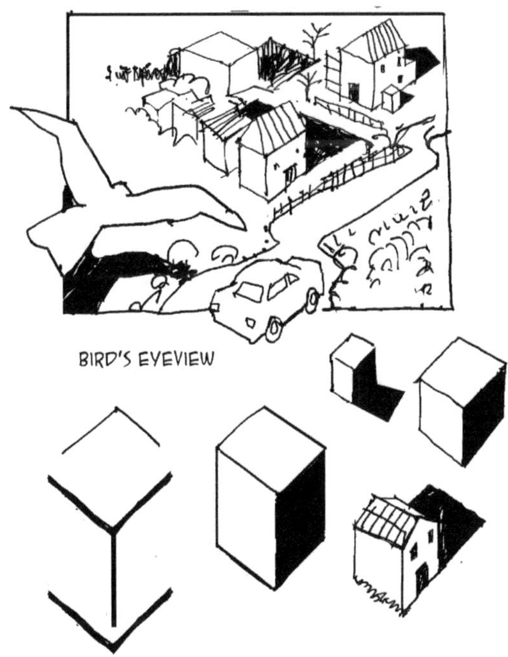

The joke is that **Y** is a crooked letter and you can't make it straight. What makes the letter a dramatic symbol is that it comprises three lines converging on a point. Our eye is drawn to the point at which the three lines converge; we are drawn in.

Imagine the bottom line as a road that converges (and narrows) to a point (that is, another line) which we call the horizon. The horizon is where the earth, a large ball or sphere, dips away and out of view. That achieved, we are almost ready to draw in the third dimension.

When we start drawing, we tend to draw flat images without any volume. What do I mean by volume? Volume is how much space an object occupies. When we look at a box, or buildings, we know we have to find a way around them. These structures have a *far side*.

Follow the progress of the simple pictures that illustrate this idea. Copy them and observe how they begin to jump out at the viewer by the addition of the far side. There is something *behind* what is *in front*. There is a shadow of the object.

Now approaching that third dimension, your perception of everything begins with where you stand and everything around you. Early on, you measure your reach to everything else. So we ask: how far is the salt on the table? Is it within my reach, or do I have to ask for it to be passed? Crossing the road, I see a car coming my way – is it safe to cross? And so on.

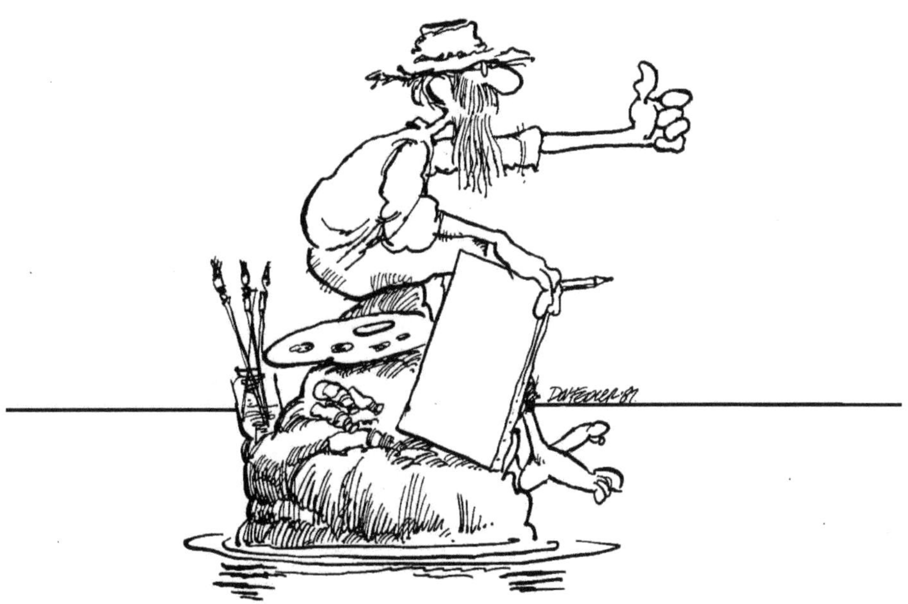

Distance here is the key. You *are* at point **A** and, indeed, you are point **A** from which everything else extends. The world is three dimensional, although a drawing exists on a flat surface. Similarly, a photograph appears to exist in the third dimension – though that, too, is an illusion.

There are many components to that illusion. Depicting the real world requires a few tricks of illusion. As we have seen, one is the juxtaposition of light and shadow.

For our purposes, an object occupies space and we see it by the way light falls on it. If the object is solid, it stands as a barrier to light passing through it. Light moves from one point to another. If the sun touches an object, that object will be lit in a certain way. In darkness, light may come from another source – a candle, a torch, a lamp, moonlight.

Perspective is the primary tool for heightening the illusion of the third dimension.

Light and shadow are a result of understanding perspective. Light on an object casts shadows. Consider the word 'cast'. Cast, as in a fisherman casting a line, implies throwing something across a distance.

Distance equals space, which only occurs in perspective.

Examine this picture of human figures. By the placement of the figures, we know which is nearer and which is further away. The closer we are to things, the larger they appear; the further, the smaller they appear. Perspective is based on the point of view of the observer.

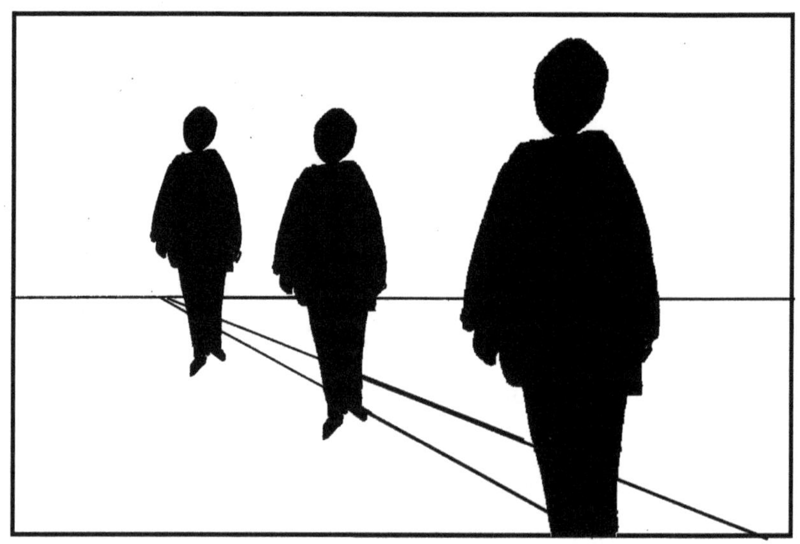

The easiest illustration of perspective is what you see by looking down a long, straight road. If you are attempting to draw such a vista and become confused, do not hesitate to return to the alphabet and the letter **Y** – your portal to the third dimension.

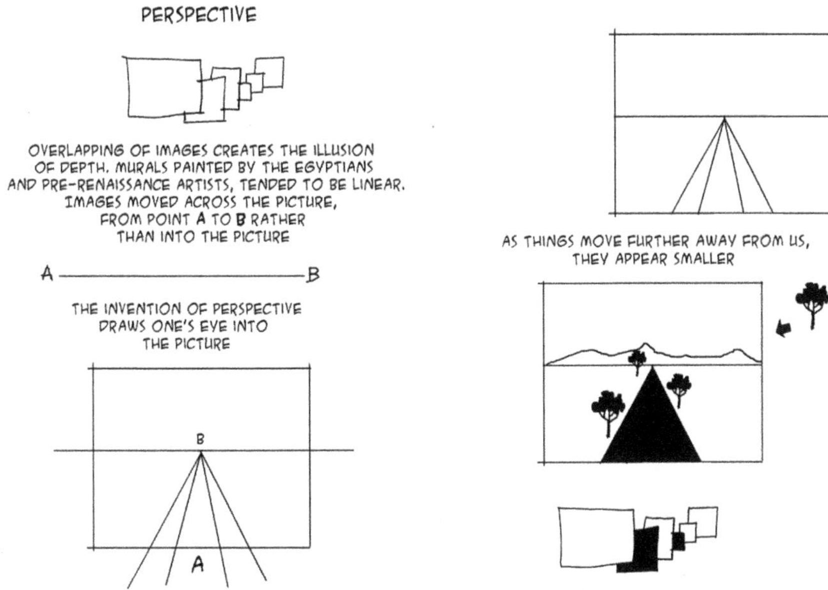

Perspective is the result of our understanding that the world is round. At the turn of the twentieth century, there were still people who insisted that the world was flat. They believed that people could sail to the edge of this earthly plane and fall off it into an abyss. For them, the truth of the earth's shape was shrouded in myth, as were the heavens. They thought of the sky as a great inverted goblet. Space did not exist – stars were little sparkles affixed to a vast bowl. Yet even the early Greeks knew better.

The ancients had scant fine machines to assist their observations. How the sun rose in the east and set in the west were puzzles that generated wild theories involving gods who presided over such motions. Still, there were those who searched for logical answers. Some observed that when a ship disappeared over the 'edge' of the world, the very same ship was able to return; so clearly, there was no edge. If, then, the earth was no more than a flat plate, one should be able to observe a ship travel hundreds of kilometres across a flat sea until it became a mere dot, until we could see it no more.

But if you've ever watched a ship forge out to sea, there comes a point when the vessel suddenly disappears from sight. That point occurs when the earth itself curves out of sight. This fact trashed the edge-of-the-earth theory. What was the logical explanation? The earth had to curve at that point.

This led to the ultimate discovery that the earth was essentially a ball. One can only see one side of a ball; the other half curves out of sight. That fact led finally to the observation that the earth orbited the sun.

The closer we look, the more we see. This applies to art as it does to science. When you observe more, you will understand more. This can be demonstrated by simply sketching out these profound discoveries.

I've storyboarded this on the opposite page. Seeing something (i.e. the ship disappearing) is different from observing. Observing is seeing plus thinking. This is the combination that leads to hypotheses and theories, and ultimately, discoveries.

The line that stops us seeing beyond the curve of the earth is the horizon. If you were in a boat following another at the same speed and distance across a vast sea, the foremost vessel – the one in front of you – would always be approaching the horizon, yet never quite getting there. The simple observation that things disappear at the horizon is the primary rule of perspective – no matter where you watch. One's eye level is always at the horizon.

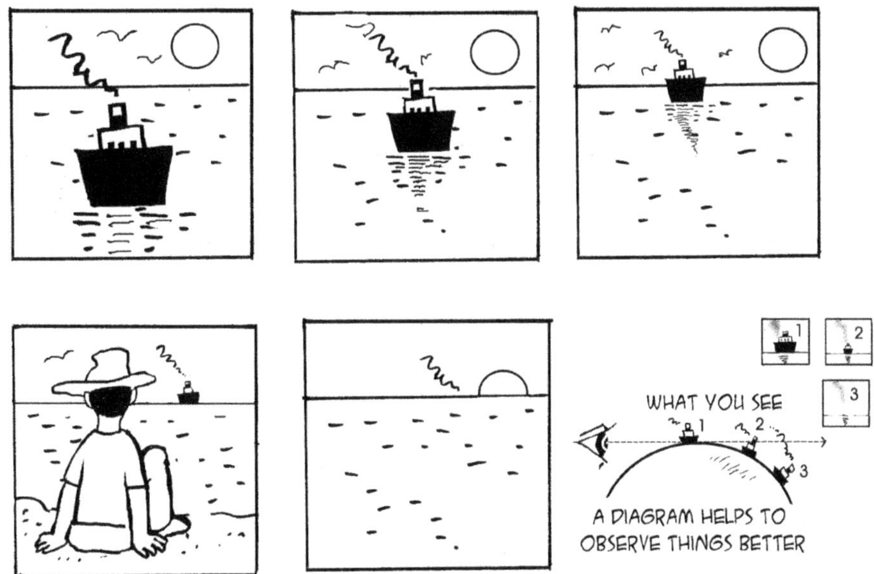

To recap: if the earth was not round, the disappearing ship would grow smaller and smaller until it was nothing more than a dot. That does not happen.

There is a point where the ship, or indeed, the sun, seems to sink.

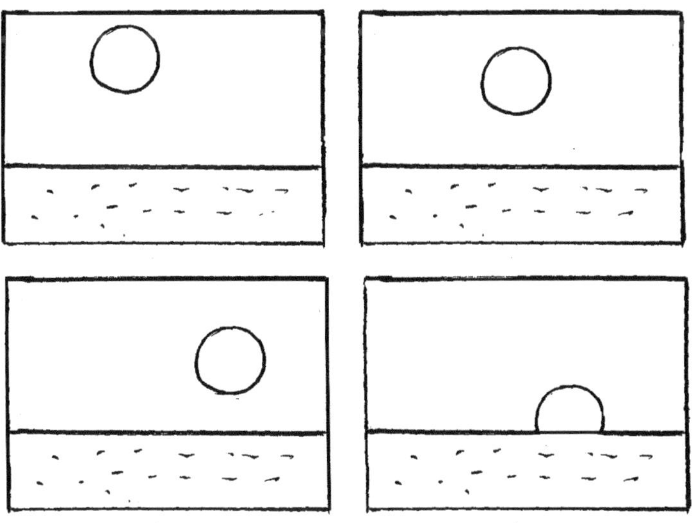

Light and shadow create the illusion of space in a picture – simply illustrated by placing a white square over a black one, as shown earlier. The illusion can be carried into typography to invest a letter with solidity and importance. But remember that an object never stands alone in space.

In the following drawing, we can see elements operating in a two-dimensional world. Moving into the third dimension, an object immediately suggests its relationship to a deeper reality. Think of the surface on which you are drawing as a two-dimensional space, then imagine a light on it, casting a shadow. The picture immediately jumps into the third dimension. The object and the shadow make real a connection in space.

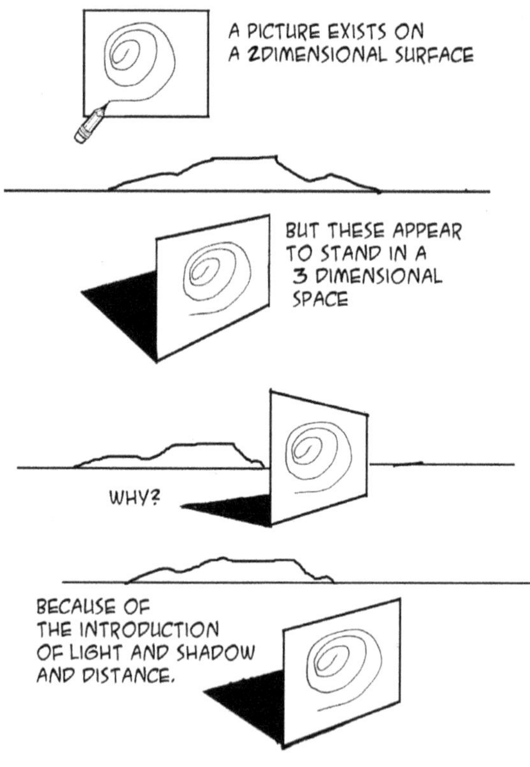

The inexperienced artist – or just perhaps a young one – tends to draw objects as if they were immediately in front of the artist's eye. By attending to the rules of perspective, you will be able to take a longer view. You will have mastered the simple drawing of a winding road disappearing into the horizon; the nearer trees are larger, and those further away smaller, in relation to your starting point. Now create your own landscapes or interiors using this lesson.

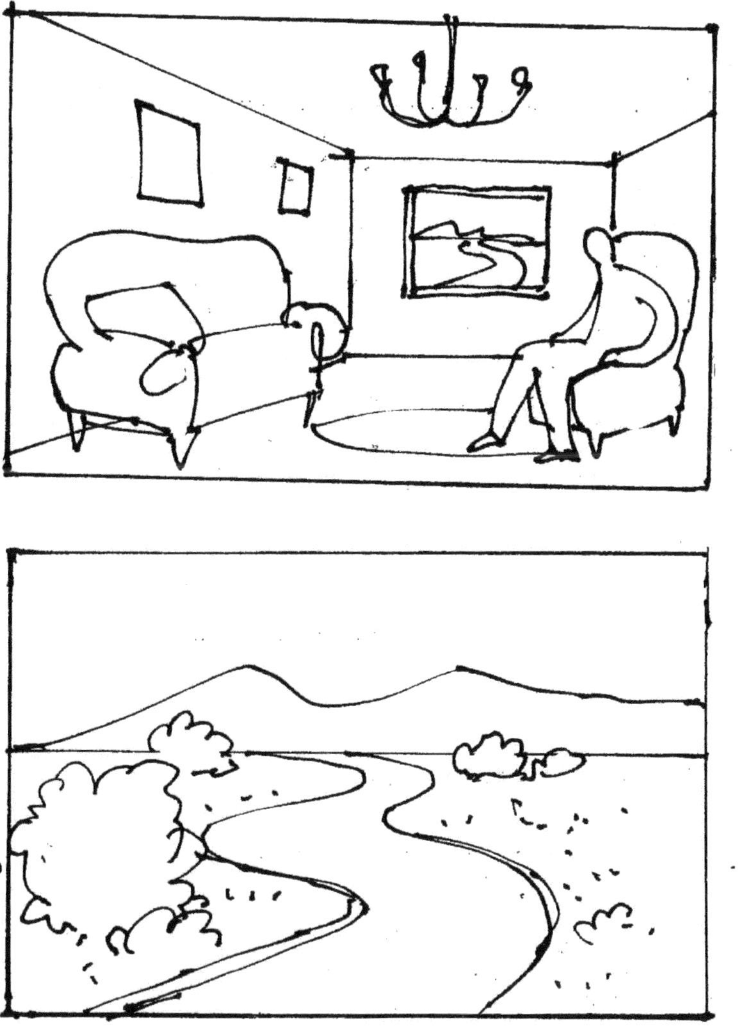

Now that you have a grasp of perspective, you can draw far more complex landscapes which incorporate the third dimension and invite others to imagine the far side.

We can now review your journey with drawings that combine everything you have so far learnt. Have a go at copying them.

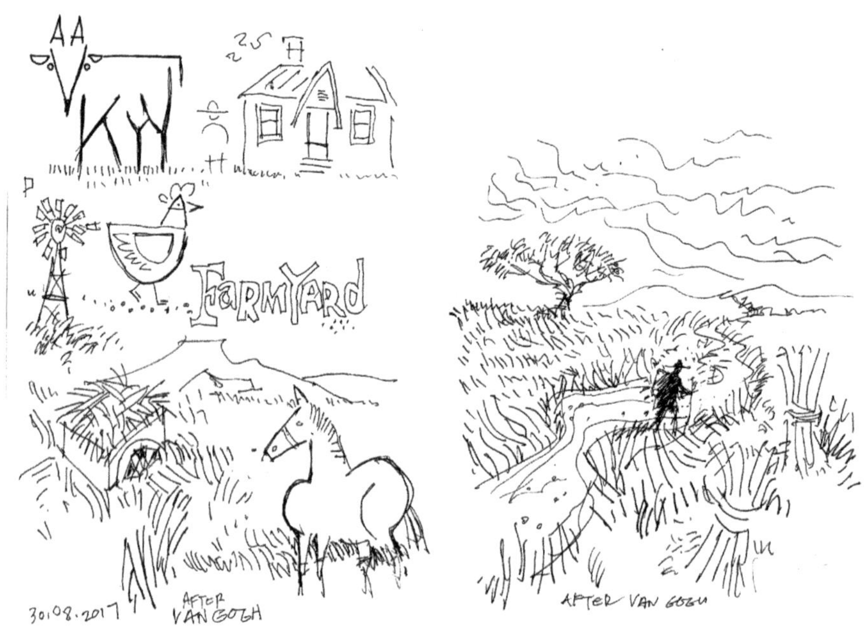

24

THE POETRY OF MOTION

While we remain inexperienced artists, we tend to draw flat figures.

To advance, we must understand motion. Early hunters understood movement well because they needed to chase their prey. This is why, although the figures of the people they drew might seem to be simple stick figures, they appear to move; they are perfect models for animators and comic book artists to employ in planning their pictures.

Seurat's work *appears* to look natural, though it is also completely designed – he drew in thousands of pixels. He deliberately did not draw figures precisely to life – but rather shaped them to an overall design, or concept. He understood the architecture of everything; even his trees are shaped to an almost geometric pattern.

The next picture is my attempt to recreate Seurat's painting using only letters of the alphabet and numerals. I have deconstructed Seurat's work to show you the architecture that gives shape and form to all drawing.

I hope you will have a go at copying this and see how beautifully simple (and richly complex) it is.

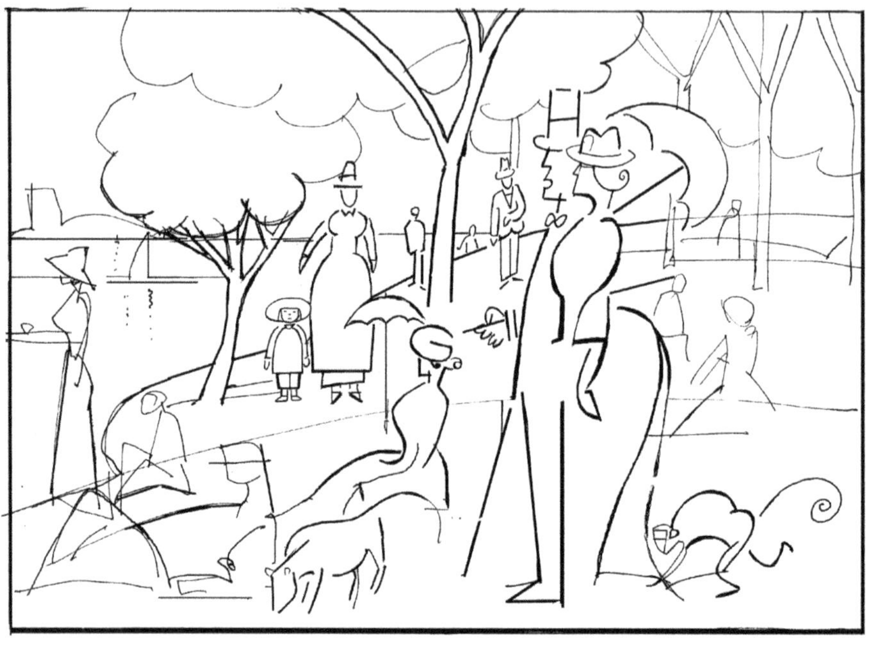

Here is a figure taken from a painting (for fun) and again simplified for you to copy.

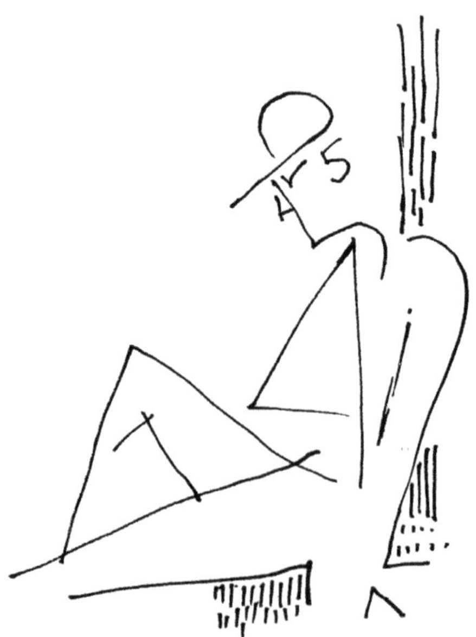

But let's move on to moving figures. Seurat's figures are solid and monumental. Cézanne was similar.

Our aim as drawers is to convey the illusion of movement in space. So how do we do this?

The invention of photography allowed the artist to examine figures in movement; and animated movies expanded on that. Animators learnt to draw figures as they moved (and computer imagery in films expanded that talent further, working through code to reproduce the human original).

Visionary nineteenth-century photographer Eadweard Muybridge produced a book of photos which became the benchmark for studying figures in motion.

Here is a sample of his 'running man', followed by the crude stick figures that animators use to develop their action pictures.

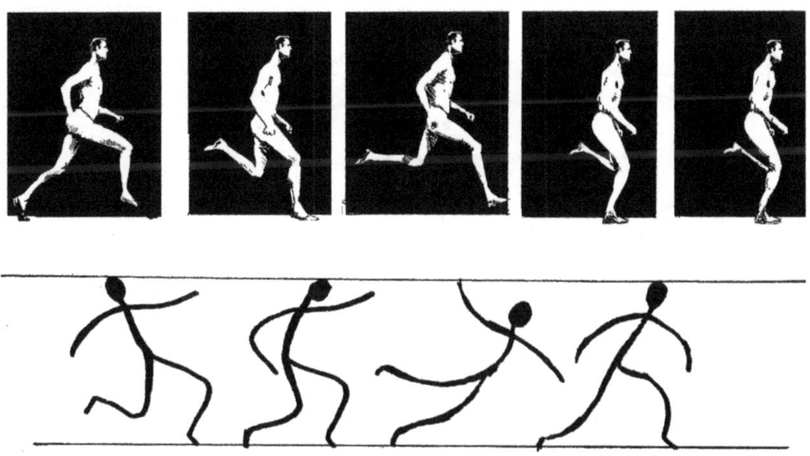

Note how similar the animator's drawing is to that of the early cave painters. This method is used in animated films and comic book art.

To really understand movement, we need to go back in time again. This time to Greek statuary, which recognised that even a standing figure is never motionless.

In looking at these statues, we begin to see that every human form is based around a centre of gravity. We shift our weight constantly from one foot to the other around this point.

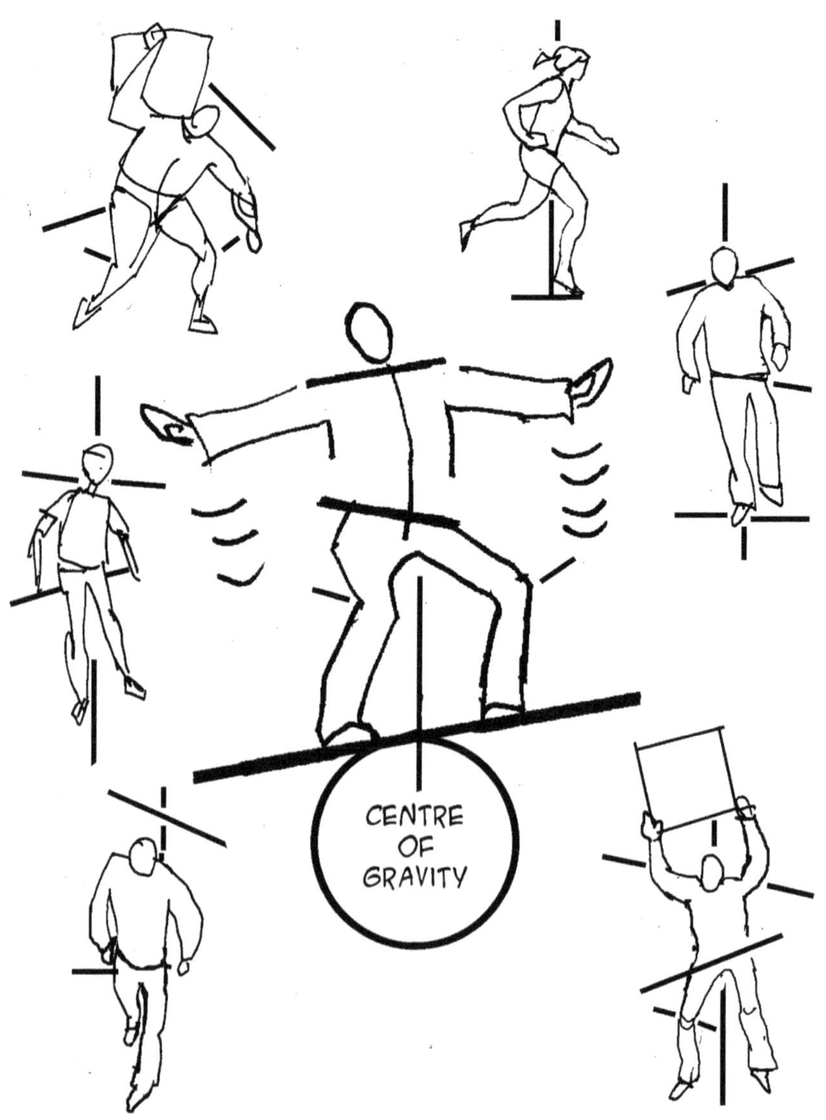

Every movement therefore has to be counter-balanced. Here are copies of two of the most famous works of Ancient Greece statuary. The male figure is the *Hermes* of Praxiteles and the woman is the very famous *Venus de Milo*: in both, though the figures are in a rested position, their weights are distributed across the body to keep it in balance.

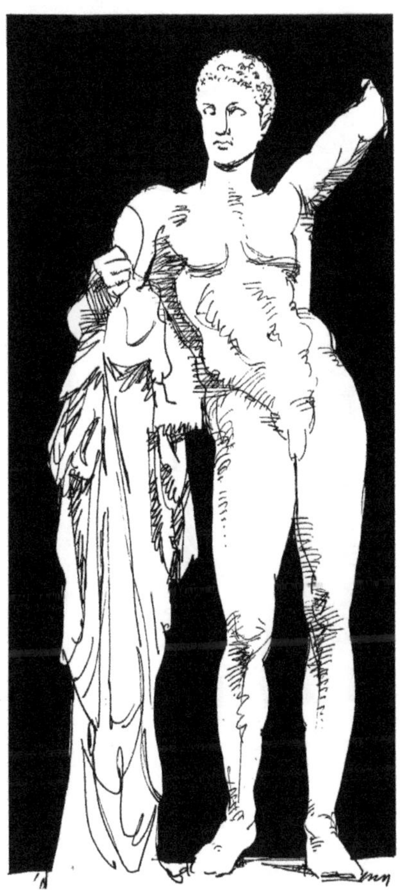

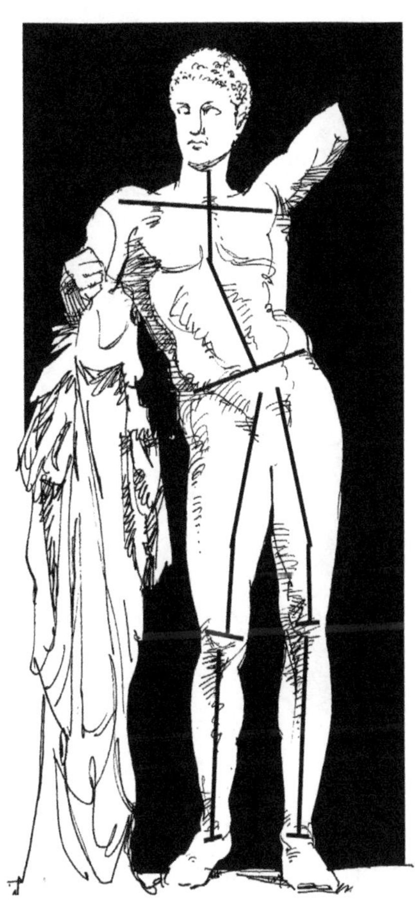

The body shuffles to find its centre line – its centre of gravity. It's this suggestion of imminent movement that gives the figures the sense that they may suddenly come to life.

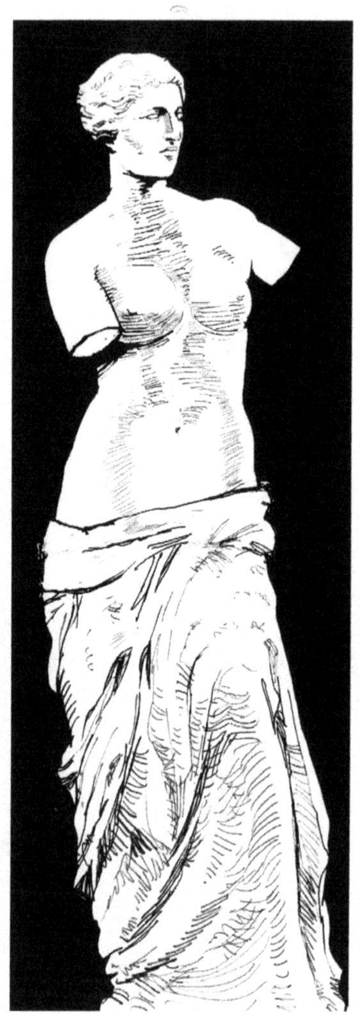

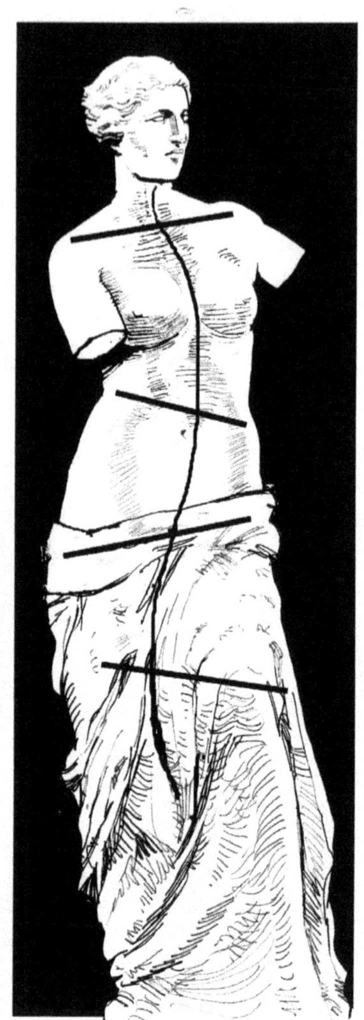

It's the same principle employed by comic book artists to create a sense of action. Have a look at how much the structure of the superhero has in common with ancient gods and goddesses.

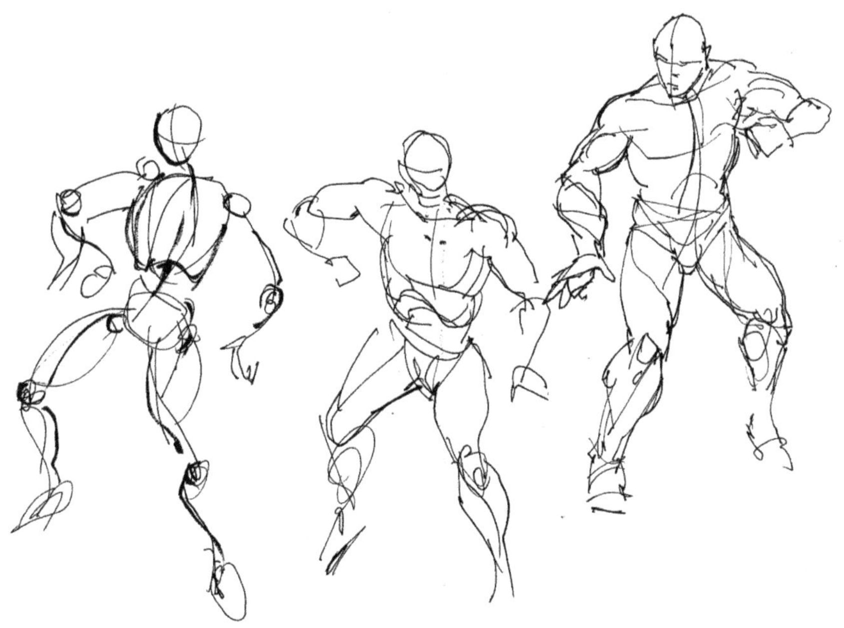

Learning to draw our figures in motion will bring more energy and vibrancy to our images.

To recap: everything moves along a central axis or centre of gravity. Creating the illusion of motion happens when we employ this centre as a fulcrum for our figures.

25

DRAWING EMOTIONS

Our next lesson is about the architecture of feeling. This is best illustrated by the use of cartoons – but its principles apply equally to fine art. Consider these diagrams as plans.

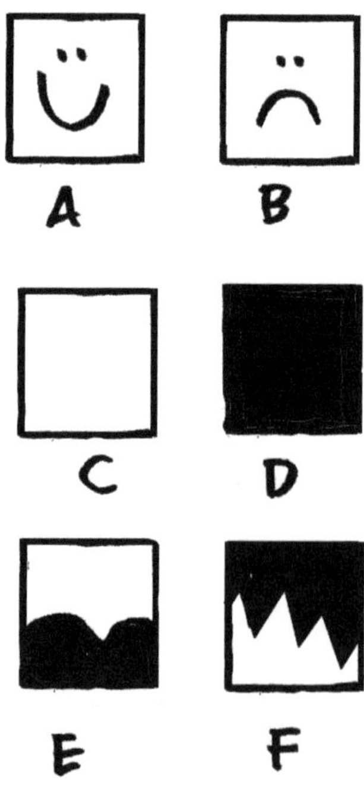

The smiley face and the sad one is not an invention of writing, but instead a deep observation about emotion. When we are happy, our mouths turn up – our faces register a smile. We throw our hands up in the air as an expression of joy. When we are sad, everything turns down – even our shoulders sag. When we grieve, our mouths turn down; our shoulders droop. Joy reaches upward and sadness drags us down. Emotions are shown in the posture of the figures below.

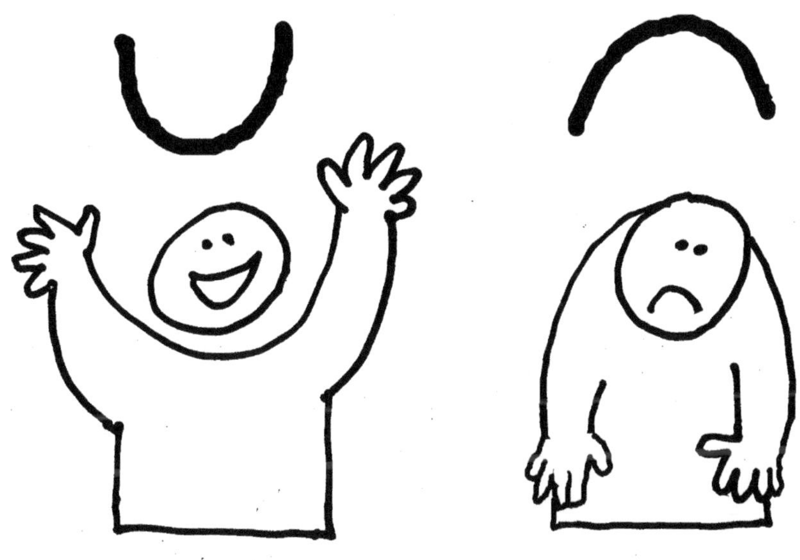

Study this copy of Edvard Munch's *The Scream* (one of the most famous paintings in art history). Note that in Munch's picture, the angle of the background dips down – and further unsettles our innermost feelings.

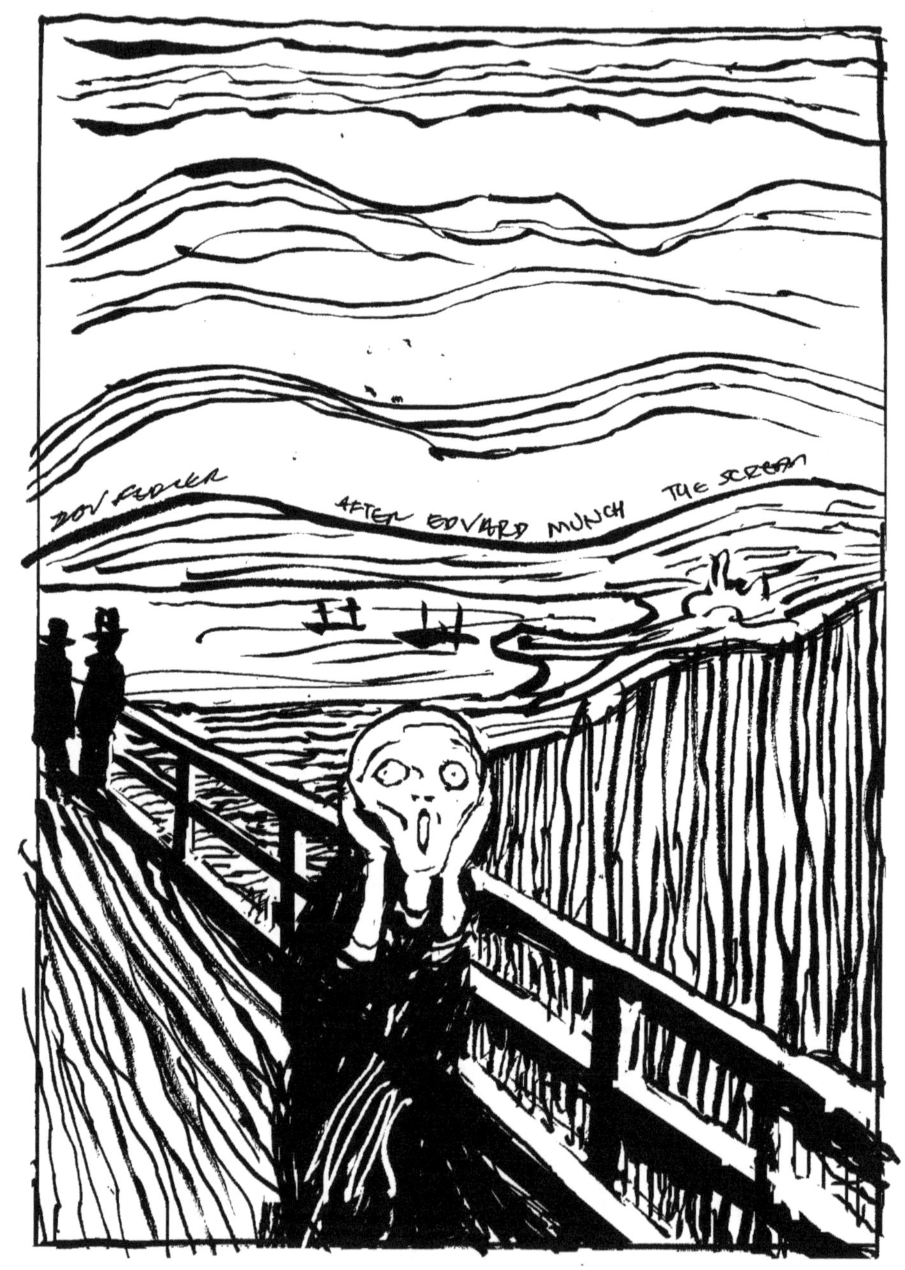

Both Munch and Van Gogh provoke revelations about our relationship to the very images that shape our inner world and tell us so much about the intricate structures of our emotions.

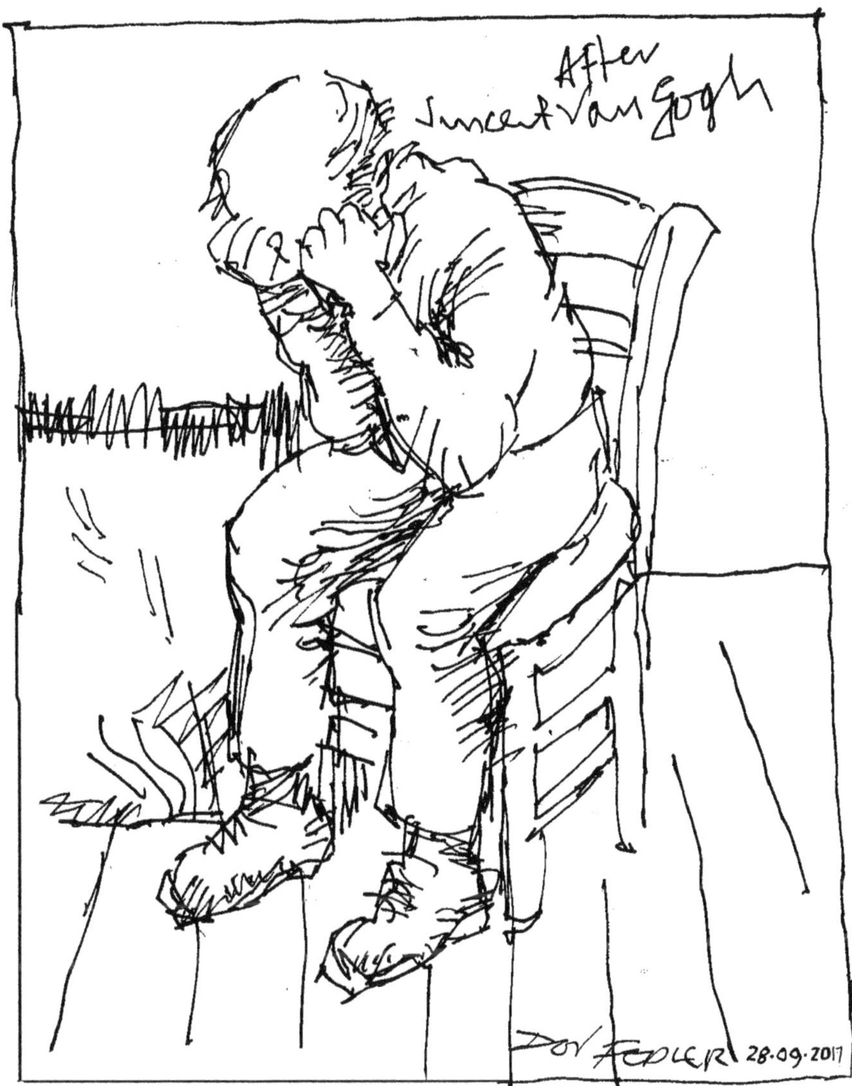

THE THRESHOLD OF ETERNITY MAY 1890

In this copy of Vincent van Gogh's *The Threshold of Eternity*, we feel the essence of sadness because of the shapes on the page.

Happiness can be expressed as a line and so can sadness, even though they call up opposite feelings. When we draw, happy and sad are exact visual opposites. This is why even our physical responses to emotion are geometrical (on the page).

Draw a happy, then a sad picture of your own. They need not be more complex than a diagram. Do you find that your happy lines move upwards and your sad ones sink down?

Let us substitute curves with arrows.

If we exchange the curved lines for two arrows – one pointing up and the other pointing down – we see that direction also affects how we feel. A church spire reaches heavenward to the angels. But observe what emerges when we use downward-facing arrows: we descend to a sinister image that we recognize immediately as the epitome of evil. So if you want to denote the Devil, simply use downward arrow shapes. This is not a philosophical or religious observation but, rather, a demonstration of how emotion is manifested in the images we see. A drawing of an angry cat's face retracts into just such a collection of downward arrows.

By drawing, we begin to see the construction of the world – its architecture.

To put it simply: anything that aspires upward is uplifting and happy.

Anything that turns down is sad and bad.

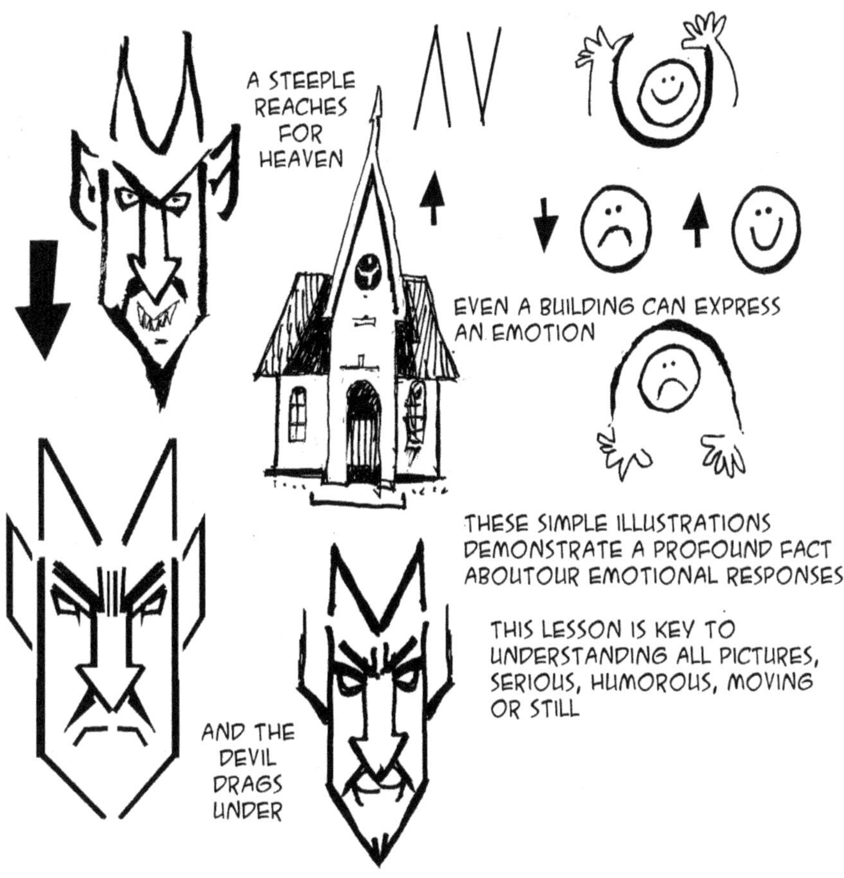

Territoriality also affects emotion. We all act instinctively to protect our space the way a lion or dog might mark its territory. For us, the nearer an unknown thing, the more our emotions tilt towards either being happy or in some way threatened, depending on how we perceive the approaching person or object. In a picture, the closer we get to the subject, the more intimate it starts to feel. If we stand back, we are more detached or removed. In this way, we mark our territory like all the other creatures.

Whatever we see evokes an emotion. A sinuous, curved line registers differently than a straight one. Straight lines have a formal quality – while a curved one is more natural. Yet the two are very powerfully linked: emotion and geometry collide and then fuse.

Our bodies are as expressive as our faces. Let's learn to draw the body in its various moods. Make sketches similar to the examples presented here, then think of your own.

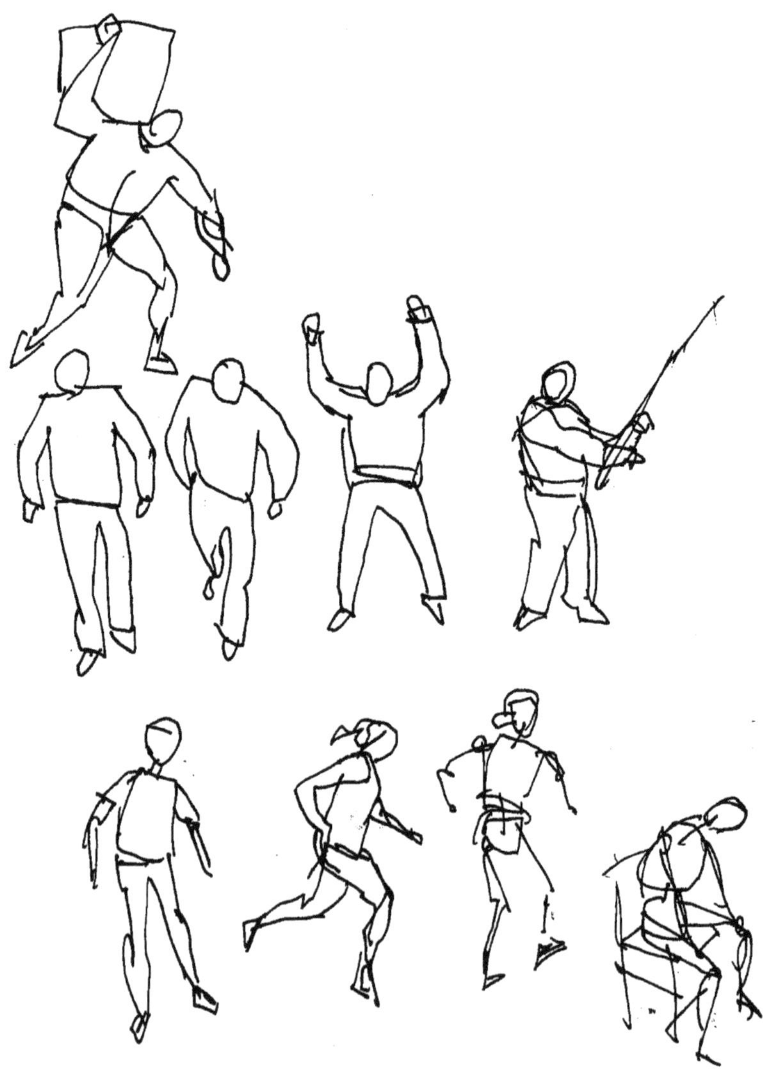

Your drawings can be as simple as the ones shown here, though obviously we seldom stand flat, as in the icons denoting toilets which we are all familiar with.

Draw figures in extreme situations – running, jumping and lifting.

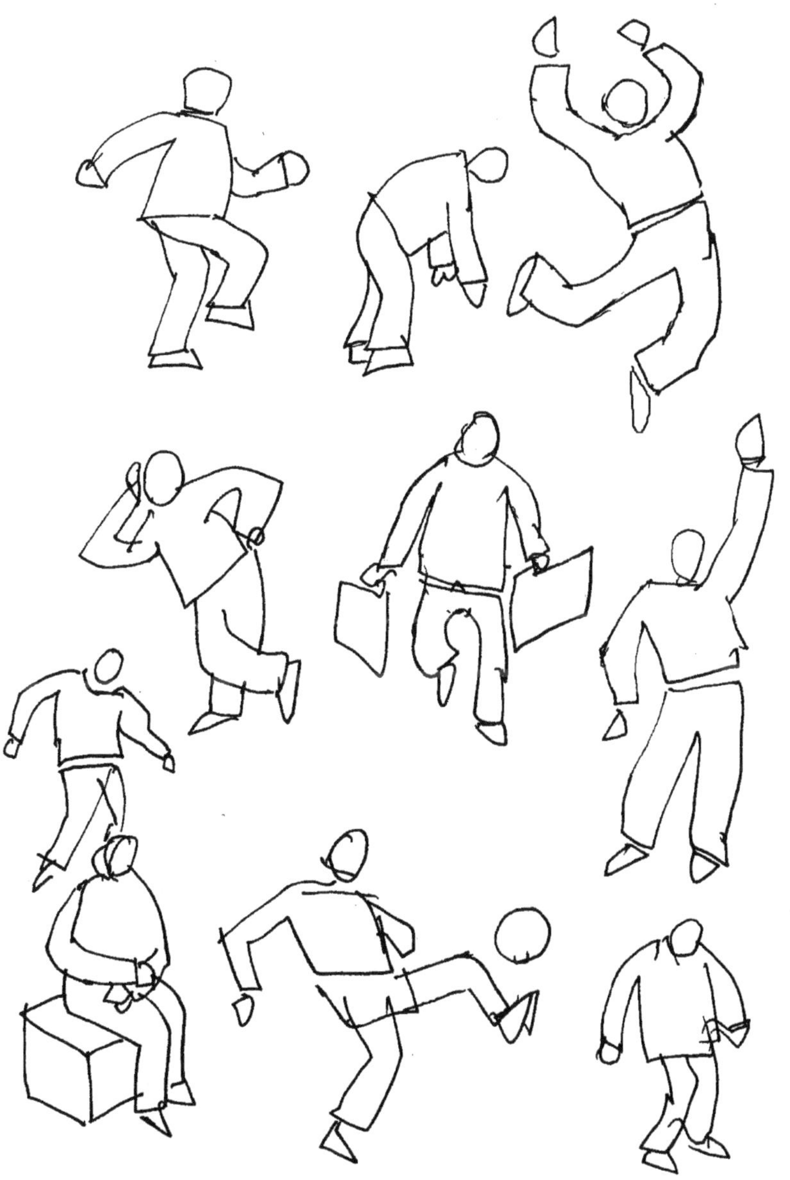

Now we can examine a fuller range of human expression. The range of human expressions is fascinating to observe. The human face is infinite in expression.

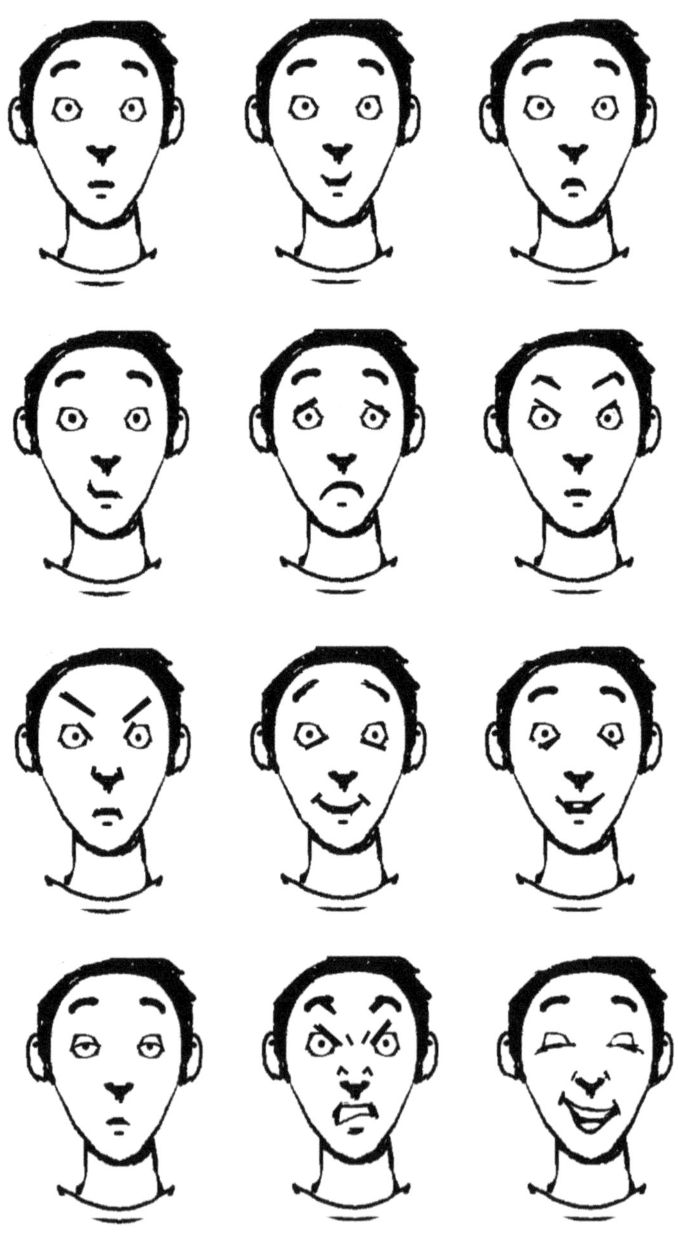

Study each one of these twelve faces. Can you determine the emotion? Can you identify any of the lessons you have learnt in this book so far? The face is bland in the first drawing – but note how the expressions change with just a shift in the direction of lines.

If you intend drawing people, copy this many times, playing with your own ideas. Then you can proceed to portraiture.

Except for identical twins, faces vary in shape and size. As we have seen by now, a face has a specific placement of components. If you visualize it as a cup, what you have already learnt makes the exercise easier.

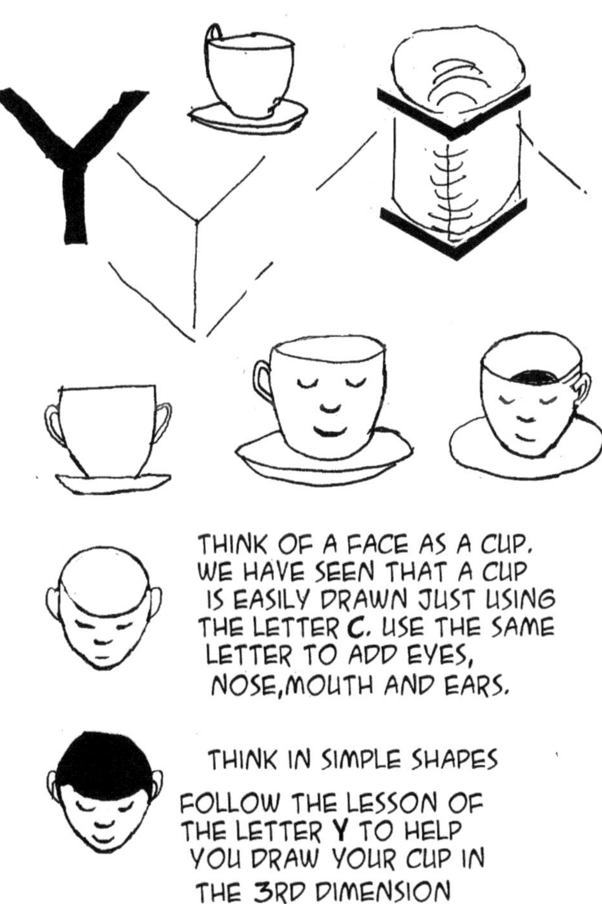

Here are some of my sketchbook pages, with a variety of overlapping faces. I've tried to draw many different people viewed from different angles – and these are informal drawings, doodles, if you like, with a range of styles and visual experimentation. That's what a sketchbook is for – it's a diary, an ideas book. The faces have been used as design elements working towards one whole.

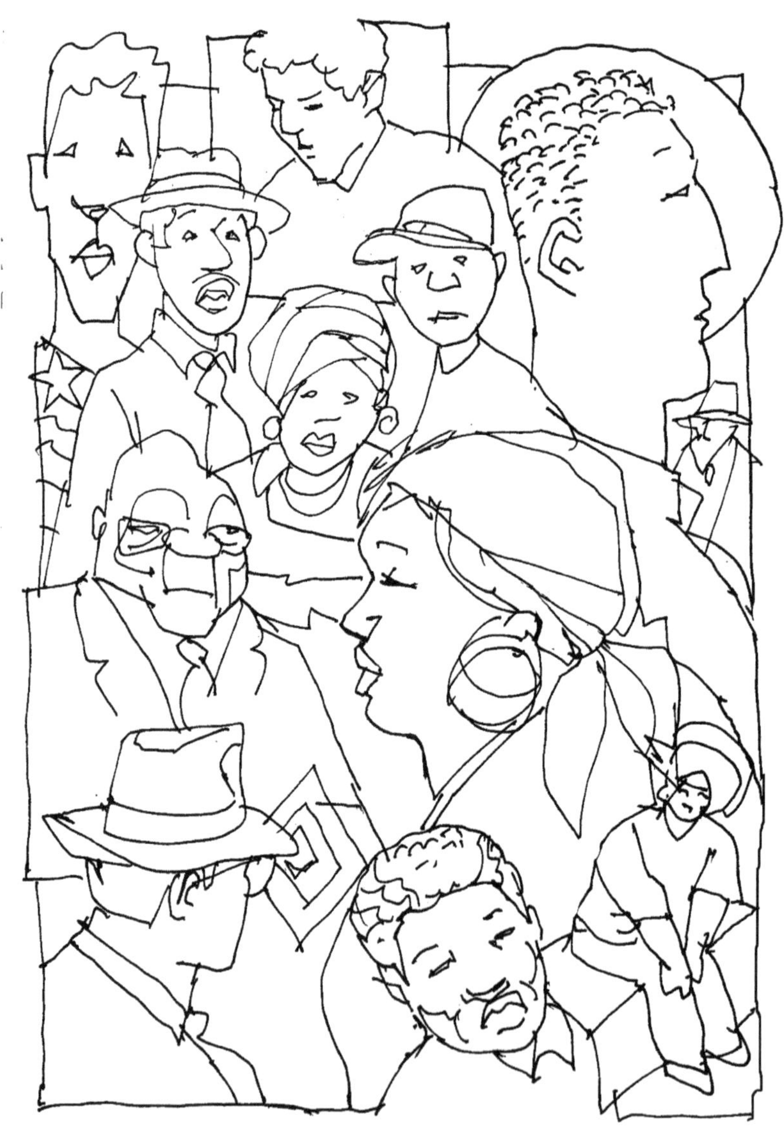

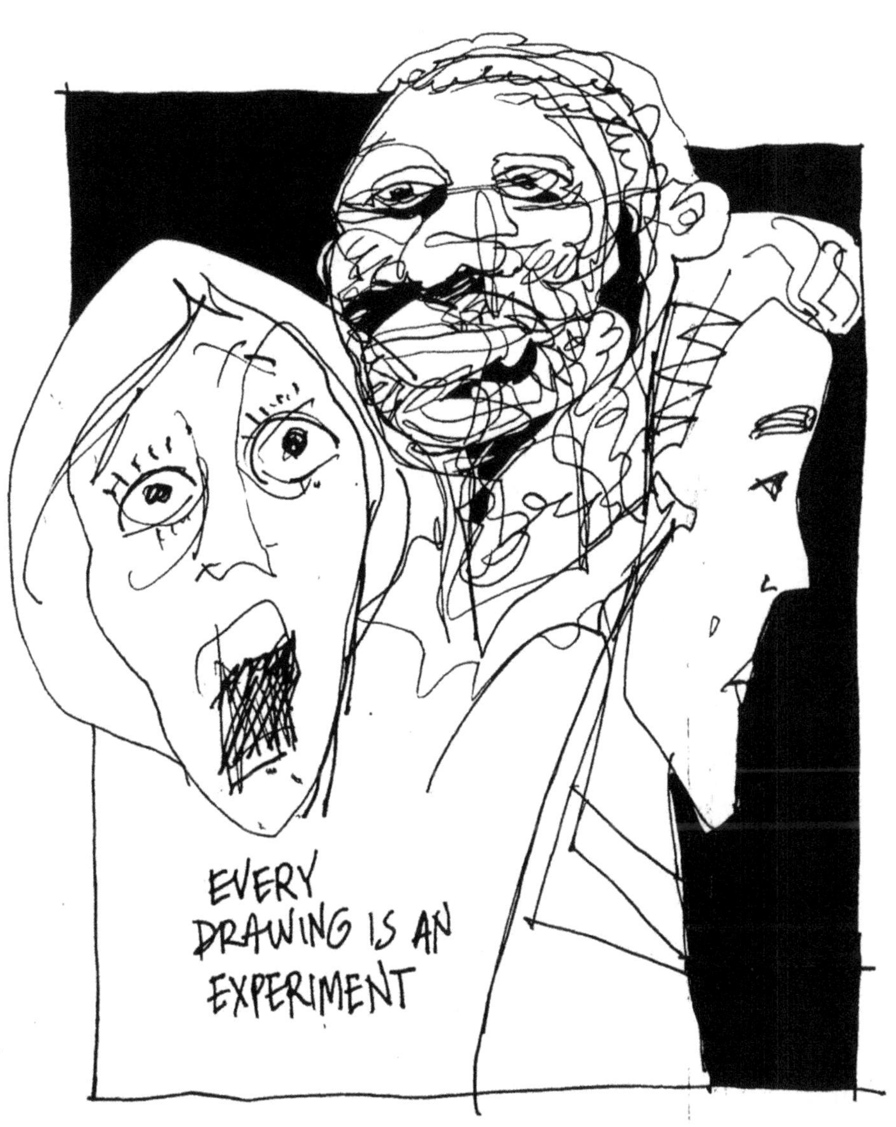
EVERY
DRAWING IS AN
EXPERIMENT

In my next picture, more figures are used – again without too closely following proportions or perspective. Play freely with it. (In cartoons, perspective is used, but 'illogical' things occur.)

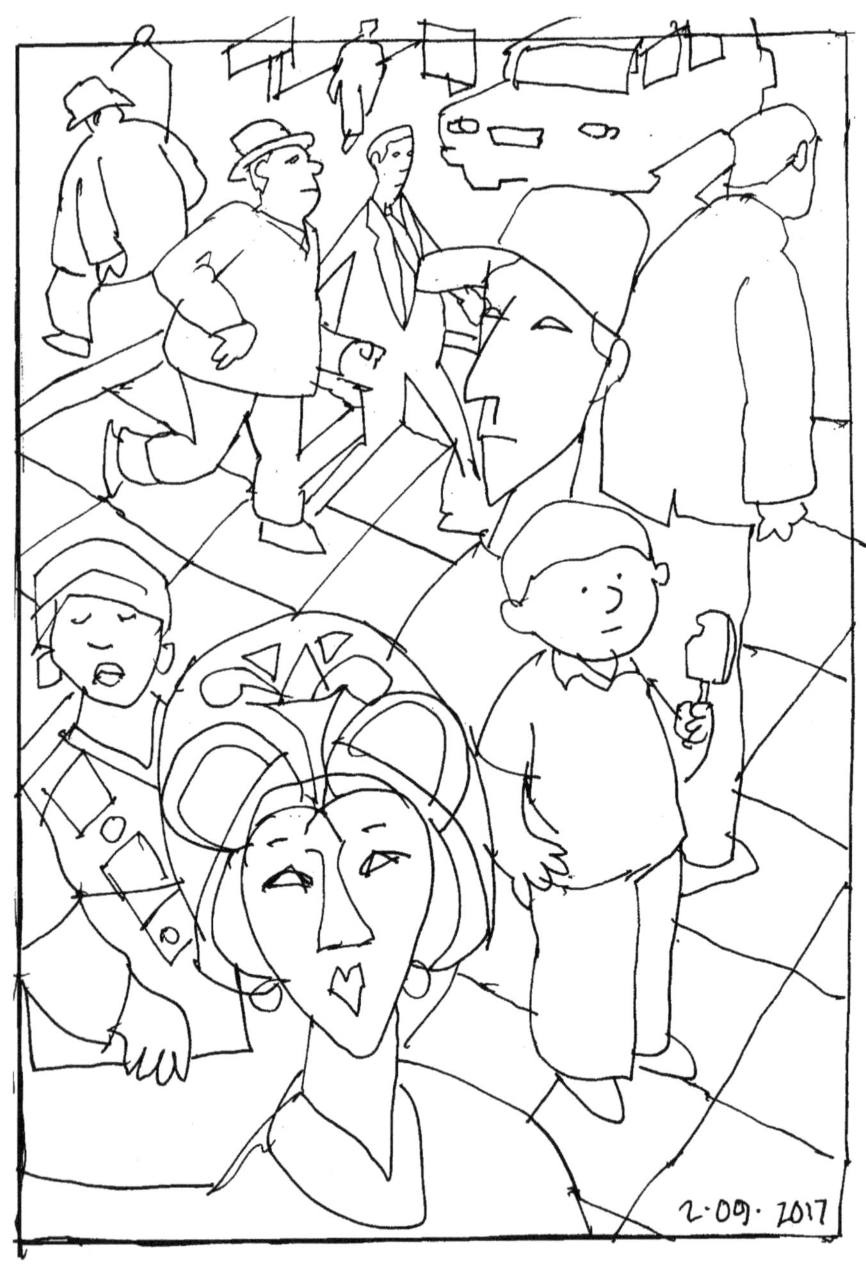

26

FRAME AND TILT

Okay, now we are moving into an even more advanced concept – that of framing and tilting to create effect.

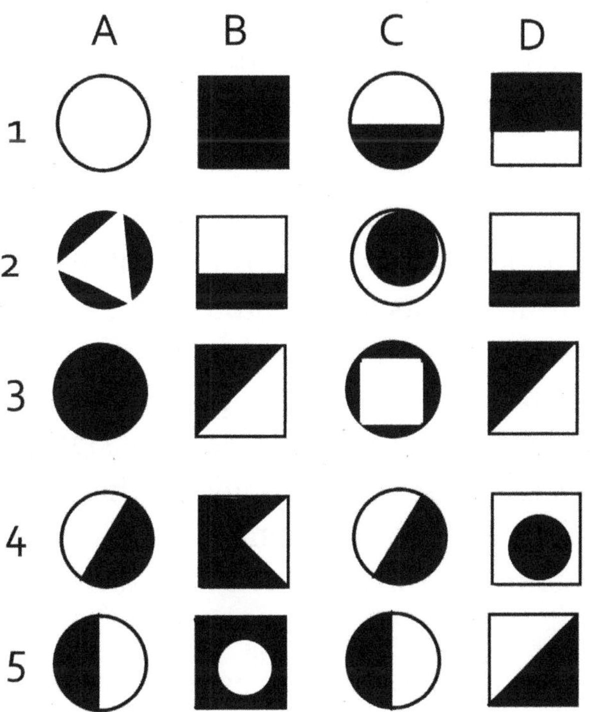

I'd like you to do an exercise. Examine the set of shapes above. Viewed objectively, they seem to be nothing more than marks on the page. Yet each one evokes a different emotion – without our being aware of it. Look at each one in turn, and on a piece of paper, write down how it makes you feel.

Did you find that you had different emotional responses to these 20 images?

In fact, we react warmly to light, while darkness unsettles us. A similar rule applies to shapes. A circle is a calmer, softer shape than a square. Did your emotional responses bear this out?

When shapes are divided into both black and white, we might have an emotionally ambivalent response. When a line across the middle of a square is straight, it is less unsettling than when the line is tilted or at an angle. And when squares get tangled up with circles, we may feel positively unsettled. Dividing the space diagonally introduces a dramatic shift in our view.

This *tilting out of frame* is a key to both film-making and painting.

When an object is immediately in front of us – provided it is not as dramatic as an oncoming car, or any situation of danger, and provided it is not too close – we focus upon it with all four 'corners' of our sight, giving its shape and incline in space to our inner mind. Our sight gives more or less a rectangular view. Yet even when we just look, we search for balance, for a centre of gravity. The second picture (the numbered and tilted one) disturbs our sense of balance.

Let us storyboard something using this simple principle

to illustrate the point. A storyboard is a narrative in frames, side by side in a particular sequence. The technique is applied in the following images, and using the lessons we have learnt in this book, you will now be aware of the emotional content of each picture.

In a film, we refer to a single picture as a frame. The same principle applies in comic-book storytelling as in a film. In fact, big movies are first laid out in comic-book form, actually called a storyboard. The ensuing example can be either a plan for a comic or a movie.

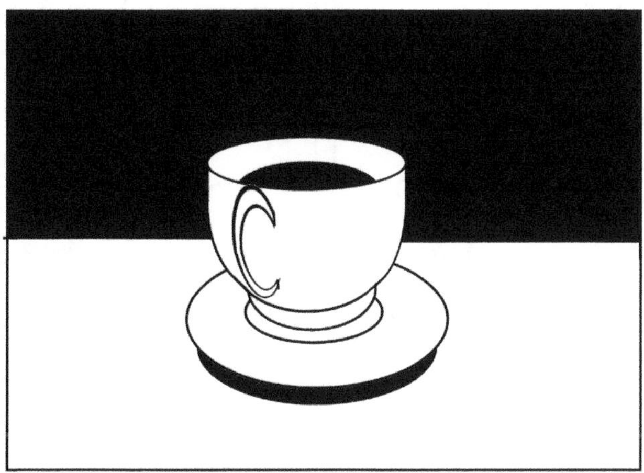

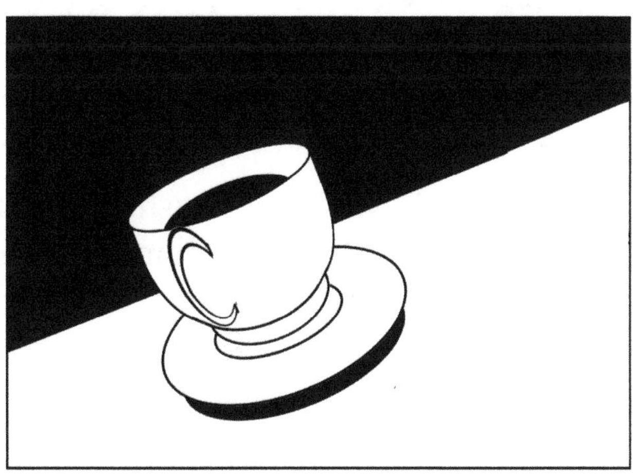

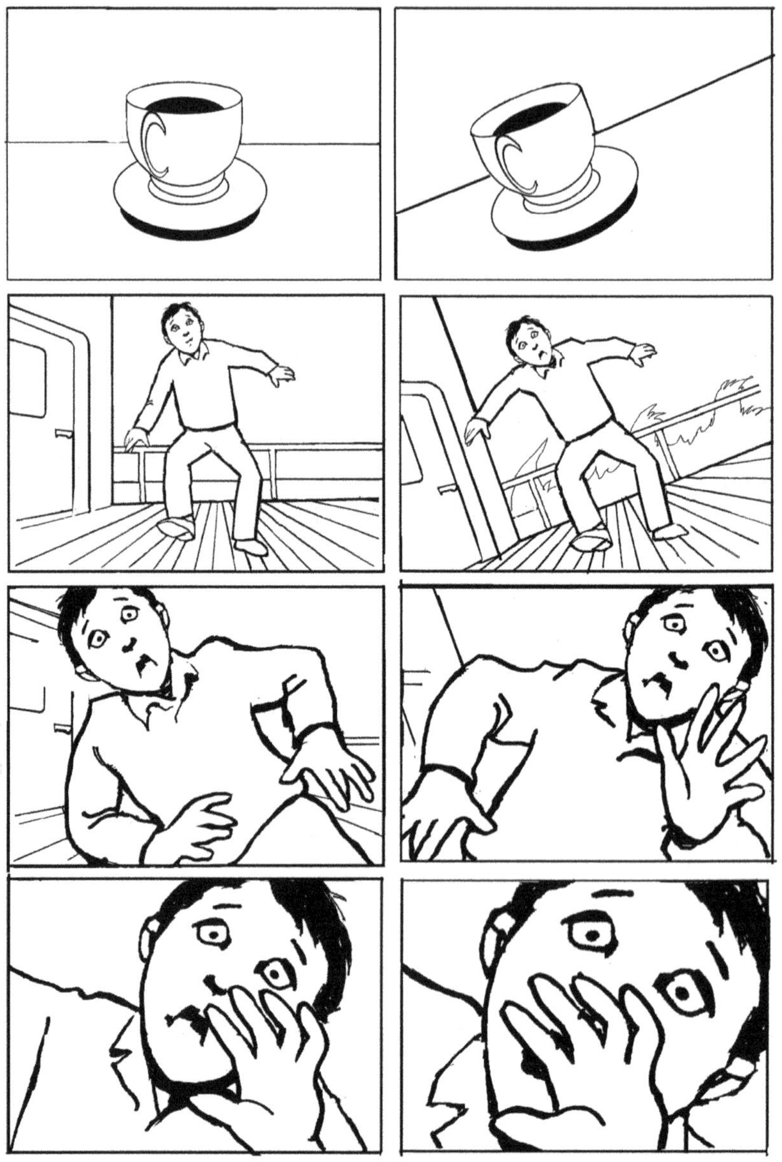

In the storyboard, we have pushed a number of emotional buttons to heighten the drama of the pictures. We will develop this drama as we go along, to highlight specific lessons.

The tilting of images disturbs our sense of equilibrium – but other details demand attention first.

The drawings have been greatly simplified to show the power of the rules of seeing. For this reason, the sequence is dramatic to a degree. The closer the image approaches, the more it invades our space, our emotions. Furthermore, we can add even more drama to the exercise by applying the power of light and shadow. Black thrusts the picture deeper into our field of vision – suggesting the third dimension.

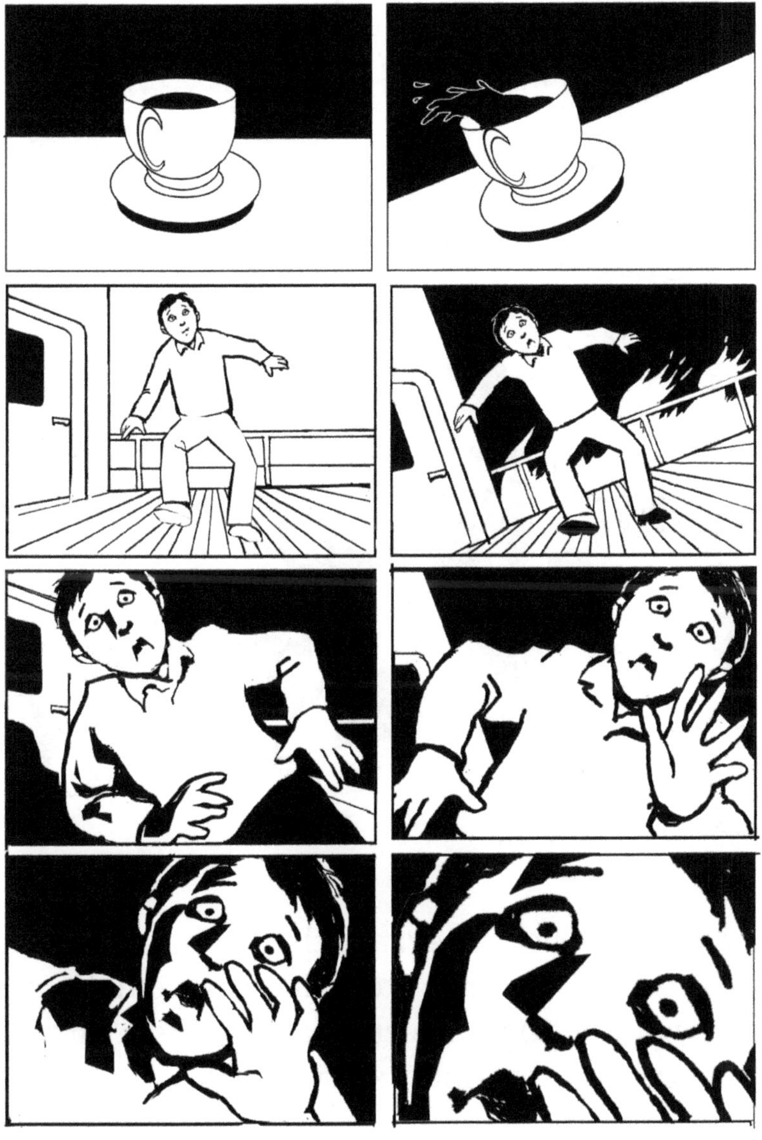

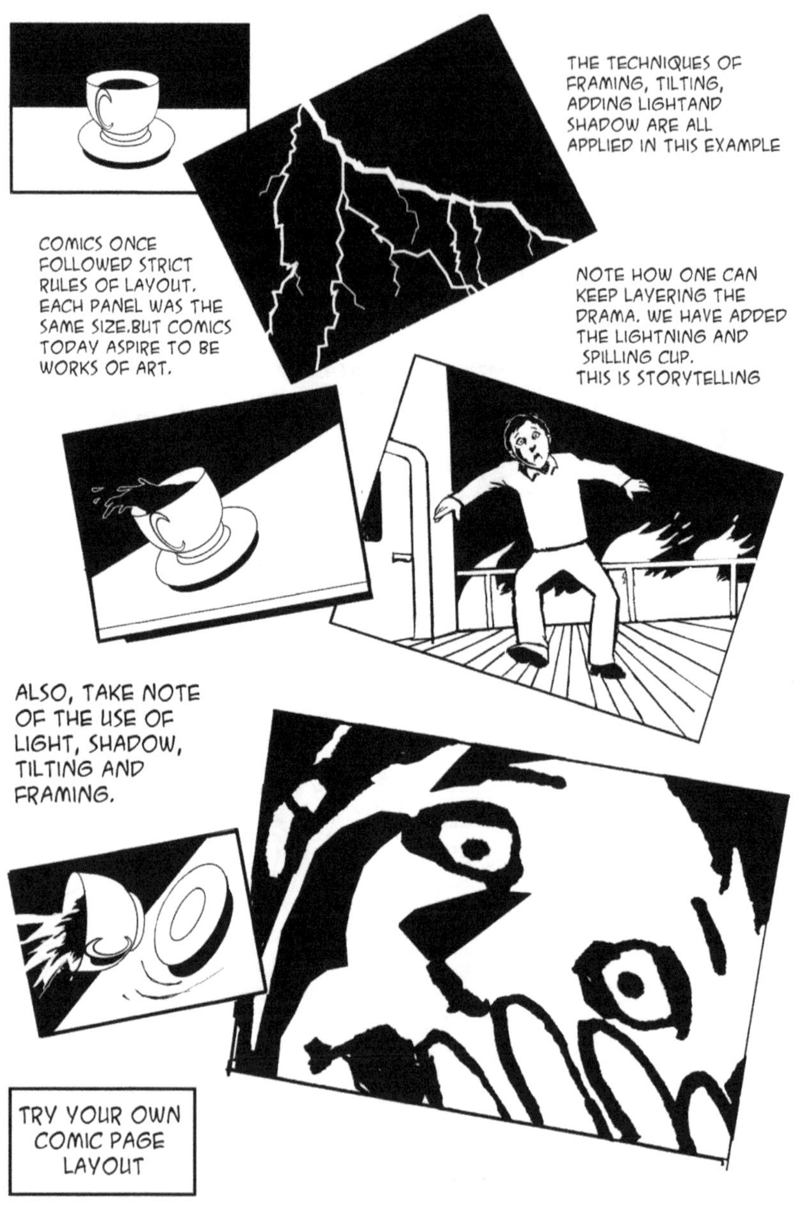

The above sequence began with the blandest image – a cup and saucer on a table. From there, our emotions were stirred by presenting the picture as seen from an angle of discomfort. A written short story – which almost always aims for just that – is born from that shift in balance. As an exercise, write the story that the pictures show.

How does one create drama with words? Here is a suggestion:

> *There was no warning of the coming squall. Had there been, no one would have left a cup of tea on the table. The flash of lightning was sudden, and the sea jumped in surprise. The whole world seemed to tilt over. The deck of a ship is no place to be in a vicious storm. Tom wanted to be safe in his cabin, where he would feel safe. He knew that the cup of tea he had left on the table would not be.*

See how the storyboard tells this story in images rather than words? Storytelling is key to all communication. Instead of literally telling the story – by just describing what each picture shows – I have attempted to bring emotions into play.

By arranging the story in sequence, we map out the storytelling in its essential scenes. But we have to think the story through its logical steps: what happens first? What happens next? Then what happens? And then?

This is why I value thinking before drawing: what am I drawing? How can this drawing work well? How can it convey the emotions I want to evoke?

All drawings tell a story and if we draw well, it means we have told the story well. In this book, I have attempted to tell the story of drawing and writing and in this way, to broaden your vocabulary of communication.

27

CARTOONS

I can't leave you without some mention of cartoons. Now that you have all the basics, I hope you will try your hand at them.

I think of a cartoon as the expression of an idea that has many layers, rather than a drawing of something from real life. I do a lot of thinking before I begin to put pen to paper and will often do a few rough sketches to get a feel for the thought I'm conveying.

I've spent my life drawing political cartoons, in which I envisage the politician as an expression of another entity – say an animal. A drawing of someone with a rat's tail, for example, shows us what I think of his views or actions. I will attempt to create a portrait of inner rat-dom. This analogizing is at the creative core of cartoons, and is the impulse that drives your pencil.

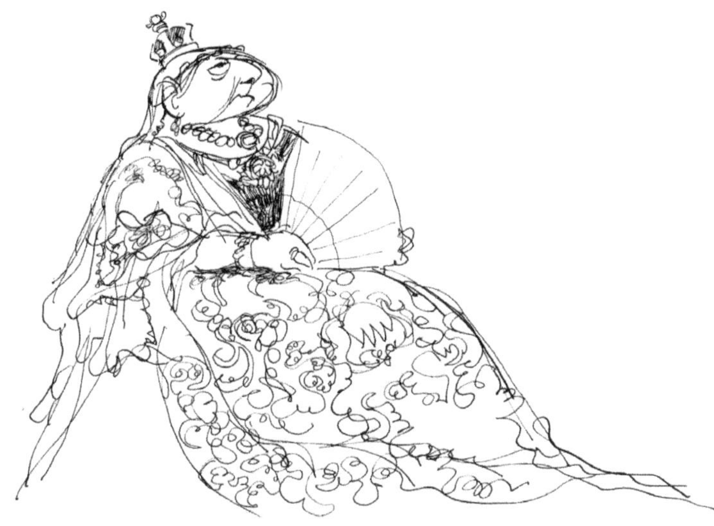

Many of my cartoons have been used in History exams, because a cartoon is also a political commentary about a time and a place and an emotion that defines that moment. From a single cartoon, it is possible to extrapolate the socio-economic forces at play in any given culture.

Here are some examples from my history as a political cartoonist.

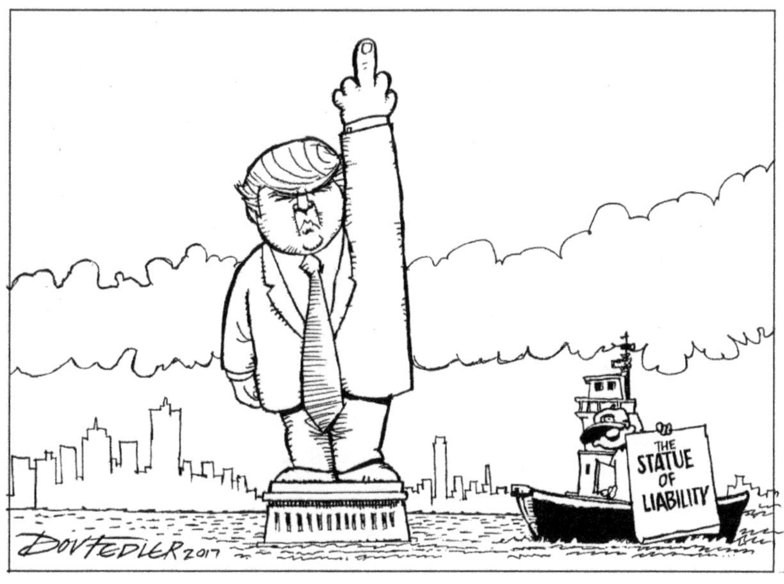

When you're drawing a cartoon, you will draw on absurdity and imagined circumstances.

Sometimes when I draw a cartoon, I want people to think. I want to expose an injustice.

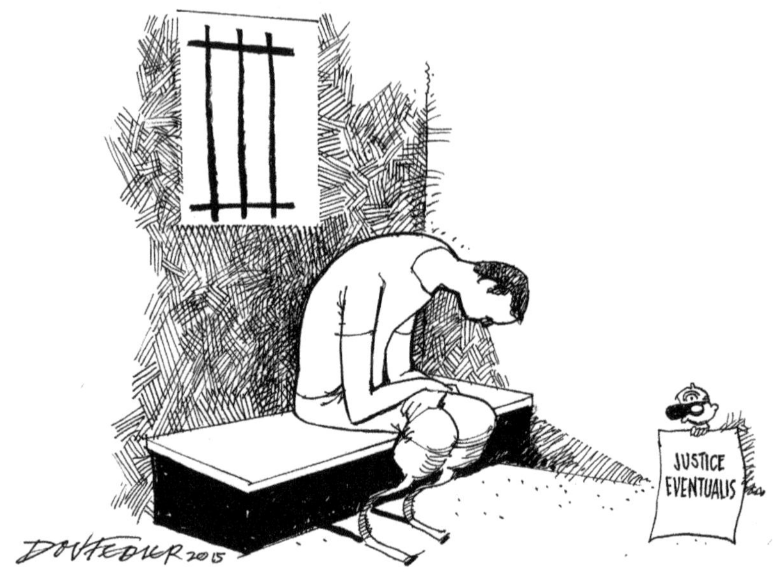

I want people to get angry. I want them to feel sad.

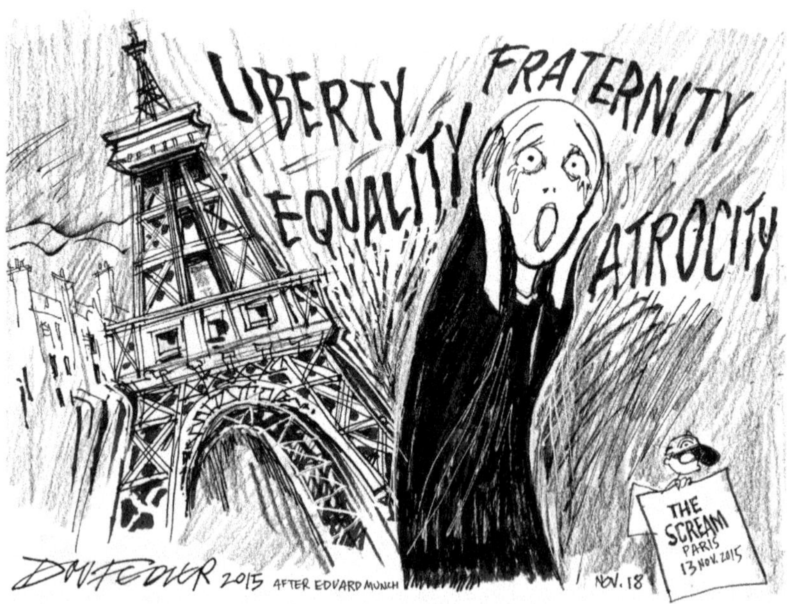

Or sometimes, I want to make them laugh. Here's one from a series I called 'Passing the Buck'. What makes this funny is the look on the poor buck's face.

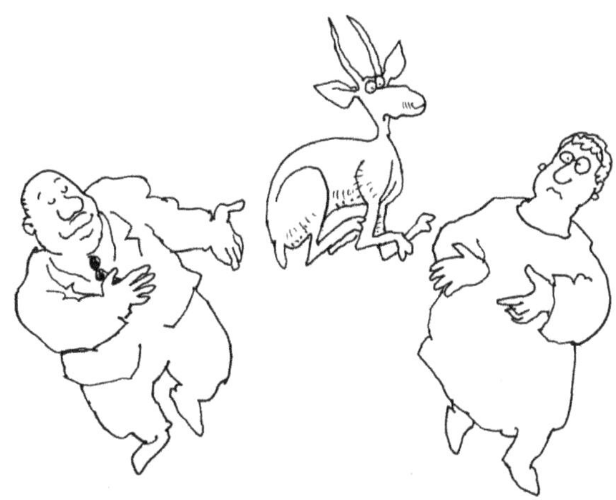

Cartoons gain force through caricature in which the character of a person is exposed. As a cartoonist, the most fun you can have is when drawing sinister politicians. I have always claimed apartheid gave me all the material I could ever need. I could draw on all the injustices to expose good and evil, self-regard and compassion in the heart of politicians.

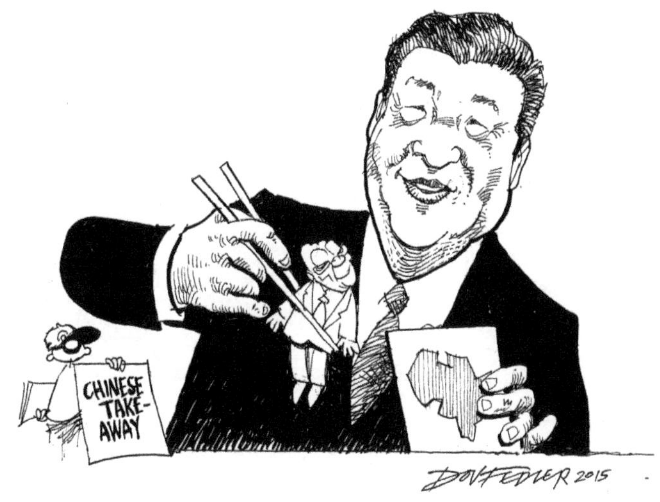

Caricature is another whole story, which relies on learning the architecture of exaggeration. That may require another whole book.

Sometimes a cartoon is just for fun – it is an expression of pure whimsy, as the Australian cartoonist Michael Leunig is so adept at.

Here are some of my favourites:

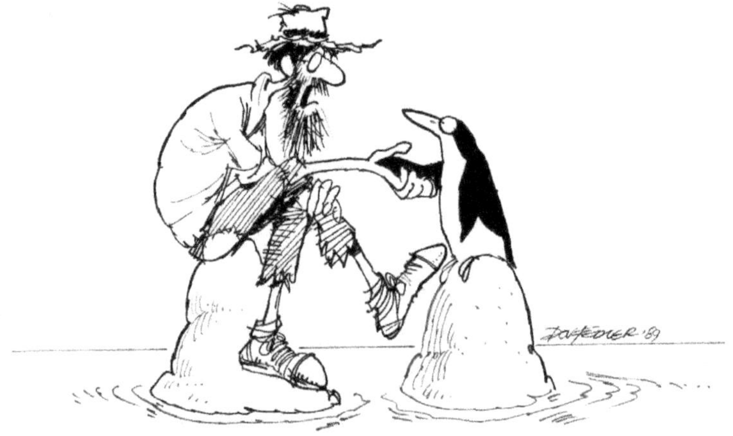

'RELIGIOUS DIFFERENCES ARE ONE THING AMANDA AND THEN, OF COURSE, THERE IS THE QUESTION OF YOUR COLOUR.'

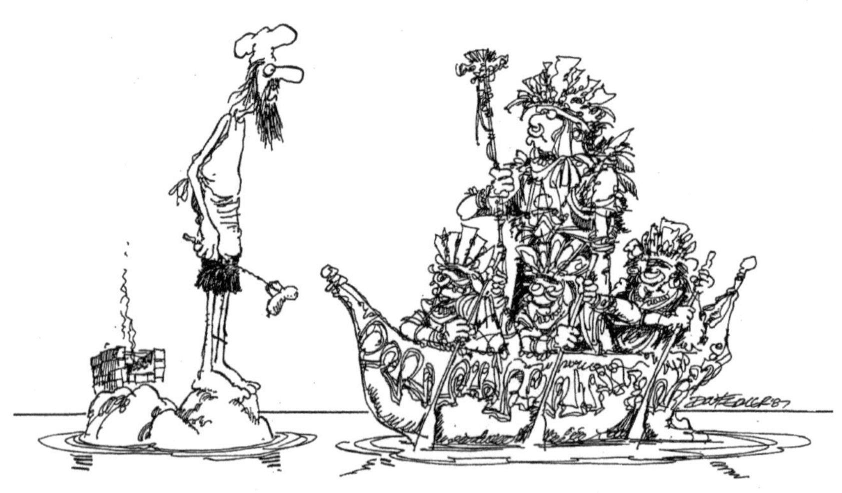

COME ON GUYS, THE INVITATION CLEARLY SAID DRESS CASUAL

Sometimes all I want is for people to chuckle and smile to themselves. Or to feel something inexplicable and nostalgic within. As artists, we draw on memory to evoke feeling – our own as well as the collective memory of humanity. Often a cartoon evokes the silliness and playfulness of childhood. That's what I was going for in this series.

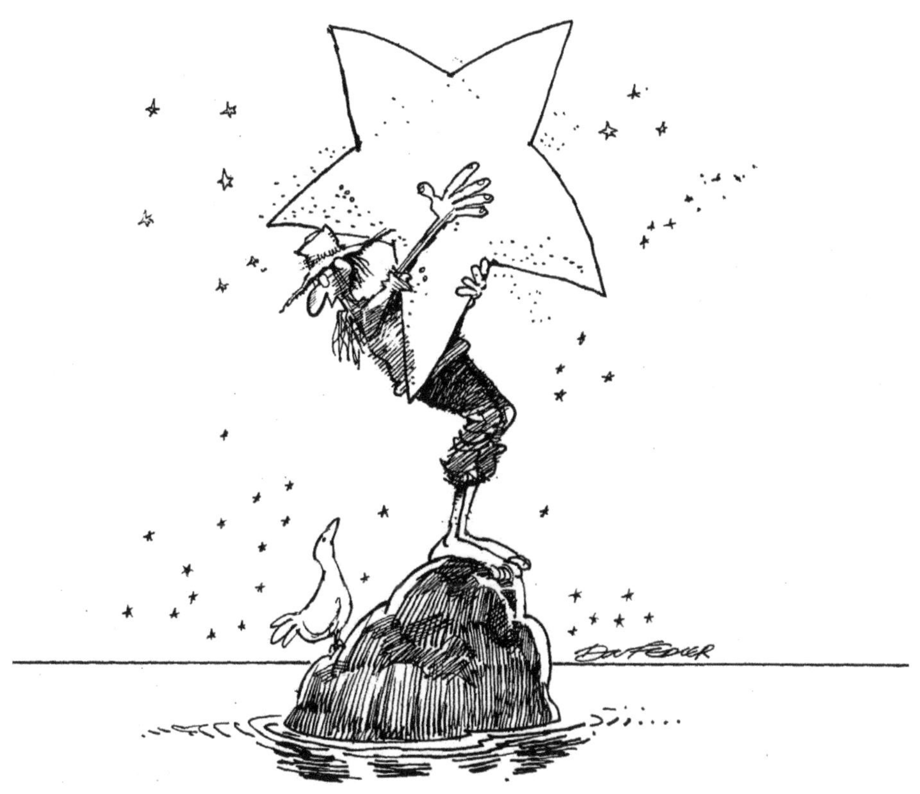

'YOU SHOULD HAVE SEEN THE ONE THAT GOT AWAY.'

Meanwhile, I hope I've given you enough to begin your journey into drawing.

28

THE LAST WORD FROM ME

We have come to the end of the lessons I wanted to leave with you. Instructions in drawing are as infinite as the thoughts that constantly stream through our minds. There is no end to learning. What I have presented within these pages is a comprehensive collection of my own discoveries, most of which I have gleaned simply from the act of drawing itself.

There are some more technical skills – such as perspective – which I've taken time to master from academic sources. Sometimes it helps to understand the theory that underpins the basics. Even so, it may take many years for the lights to go on, as they did for me with physics all those years ago.

My intention in writing this book was to demystify many of the processes around drawing and to give you easy examples to copy and follow.

I want to pass on to you the few techniques I now intimately appreciate, having spent so many years of my life with a pen in my hand. These skills now belong to you – that's how it works. Please use them well.

Finally, I hope that what I have been able to pass on to you is that it is only by the constant exploration of one's own drawings that our skill and confidence grows. Take whatever has inspired, enlivened or delighted you from these pages, and begin there. Get a pen and paper and begin your own journey into the world that lies dormant within you, the world that is always at your fingertips.

If I had to answer the question where drawing comes from and why I want you to have it as a tool in your life's arsenal, I guess it is because I regard drawing as a generous gift from some inspired source. It connects us with something bigger than and beyond us. It takes us ... elsewhere. It comes through us and is ours to play with. How lucky are we to be its caretaker? How can we ever take it for granted?

I always keep Michelangelo's definition close at hand. It is, in its way, a prayer of thanks to our creative source.

> *'Let this be plain to all. Design, or as it is called by another name, drawing, constitutes the fountainhead and substance of painting and sculpture and architecture and every other kind of painting, and is the root of all sciences. Let him who has attained the possession of this be assured that he possesses a great treasure.'*

I hope you find the treasures within you, awaiting your unearthing.

Now it's over to you.

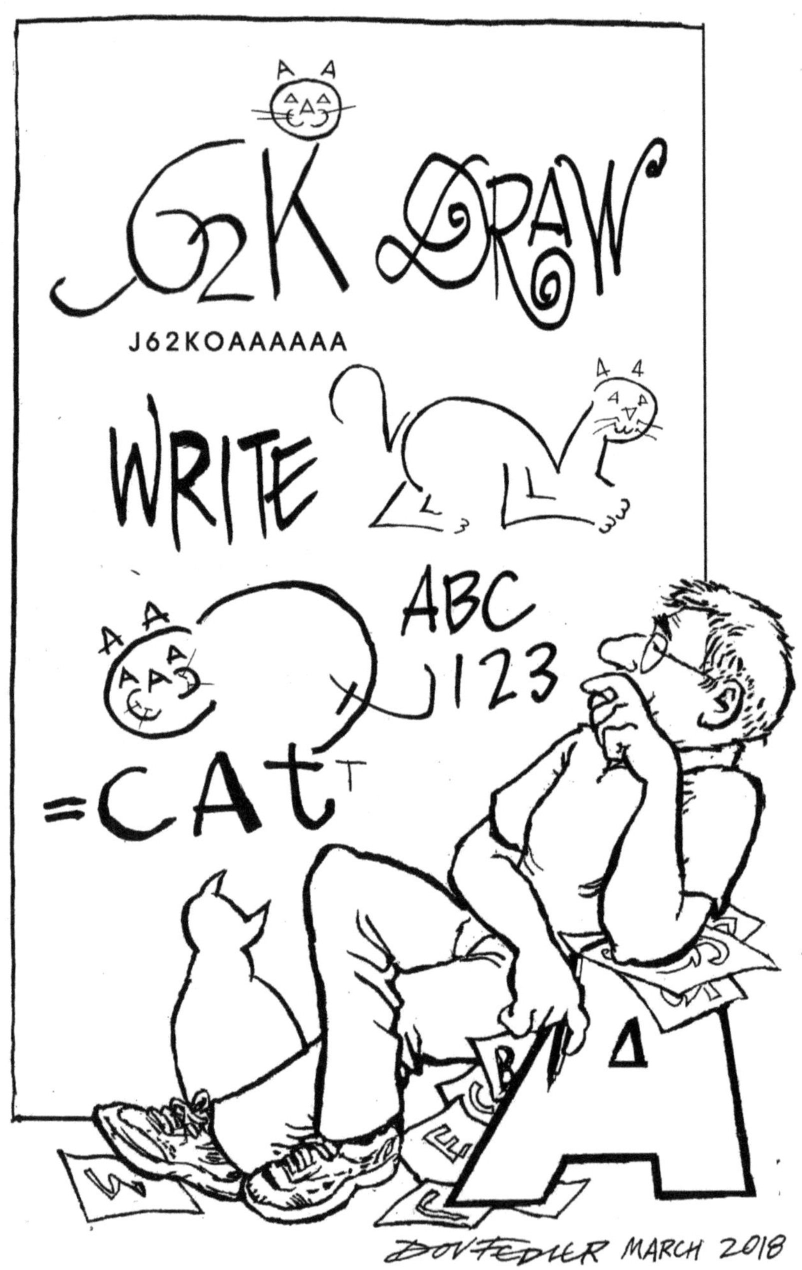

Acknowledgements

As a writer or cartoonist, one spends a lot of time in isolation, spinning off ideas into the ether with no feedback but the echo of one's ego. Has the idea got any merit? The ego declares everything to be great, like a mother who sees no fault in her progeny. It is when others pick up the scent of something worthwhile that something good begins to emerge. It is when a community rallies behind an idea that it blossoms.

I worked alone for 12 years and finally acquired Debbie Gardner as a partner who worked tirelessly to find clients and projects, market my work and run the business. In the early 1970s, I did some teaching and that's when the idea of a book on drawing first occurred to me. The idea lay dormant for nearly 30 years.

Debbie always saw the value of a book on drawing and she encouraged me through the years to get to it. She engaged Anthony Dalton, a designer, to help lay out some pages as we discussed producing a textbook. The project died with Debbie's increasing bad health. Alas, she has not lived to see the completion of the project, and this is one of my greatest sadnesses. She would have been so proud. I owe so much to her unfailing faith in me.

My daughter Joanne, who set up her own publishing company, Joanne Fedler Media, has carried this book forward to a reality, determined that I 'leave a legacy'. My great colleague and friend Peter Wilhelm was engaged to reshuffle the scattered deck that are my thoughts and to bring order to this ambitious enterprise. Joanne, who is some mean writer, shaped the manuscript further and handed it to Alison Lowry, who is a Rolls Royce of an editor, for final polish. To have all three behind me has me thinking, 'Hey, maybe this isn't such a bad idea.'

Thanks to the team at Joanne Fedler Media including Nailia Minnebaeva for adding her beautiful design to the cover and to Norie Libradilla for proofreading the manuscript - more than once. Karen McDermott of Serenity Press and Ida Jansson from Amygdala Design lent their brilliance to the process of birthing this book. In Africa we call it 'ubuntu' - it means 'it takes a village...' I am indebted to the many hands that have helped bring this book into the world.

Dov Fedler

Johannesburg, June 2018

About the Author

Dov Fedler is one of South Africa's pre-eminent cartoonists and illustrators. He retired in 2016 from *The Star*, the country's leading daily newspaper at the time, after a career spanning more than 50 years. Through his drawings, he captured the moon landings, the rise of the National Party, the imposition of apartheid, the release of Nelson Mandela, South Africa's brave new dawn, Donald Trump's election and everything in between.

He is also a sculptor and artist and created the cartoon strip Jet Jungle as well as Zibi, the iconic anti-litter ostrich that adorned every dustbin in South Africa in the 1980s.

In 2015, his memoir *Out of Line* was published and later that year he won South Africa's Jewish Report Art, Sport, Science & Culture Award.

These days he spends his time writing, rewatching his favourite old movies and plotting ways to pass the pen to the next generation.

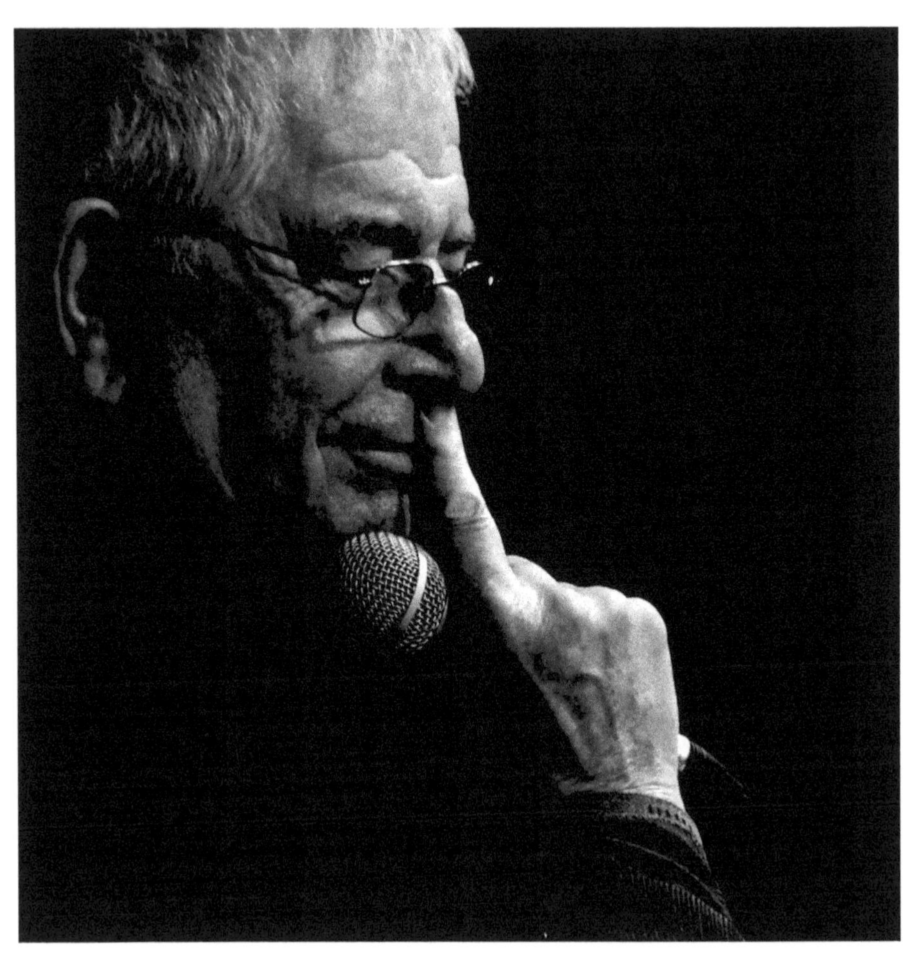

Author photo by David Batzofin

www.ingramcontent.com/pod-product-compliance
Ingram Content Group UK Ltd.
Pitfield, Milton Keynes, MK11 3LW, UK
UKHW020141250726
13967UKWH00002B/803

9 780648 283898